Founded in 1807, John Wiley & Sons is the oldest independent publishing company in the United States. With offices in North America, Europe, Australia and Asia, Wiley is globally committed to developing and marketing print and electronic products and services for our customers' professional and personal knowledge and understanding.

The Wiley Trading series features books by traders who have survived the market's ever-changing temperament and have prospered—some by reinventing systems, others by getting back to basics. Whether a novice trader, professional or somewhere in between, these books will provide the advice and strategies needed to prosper today and well into the future.

For a list of available titles, visit our Web site at www.WileyFinance.com.

Trade Like a Hedge Fund

Ben,

Good Luck

Trading

Trade Like a Hedge Fund

*20 Successful
Uncorrelated Strategies
& Techniques to
Winning Profits*

JAMES ALTUCHER

WILEY

John Wiley & Sons, Inc.

Published by John Wiley & Sons, Inc., Hoboken, New Jersey.

Published simultaneously in Canada.

For general information on our other products and services, or technical support, please contact our Customer Care Department within the United States at 800-762-2974, outside the United States at 317-572-3993 or fax 317-572-4002.

Wiley also publishes its books in a variety of electronic formats. Some content that appears in print may not be available in electronic books.

For more information about Wiley products, visit our Web site at www.wiley.com.

Library of Congress Cataloging-in-Publication Data:

Altucher, James
    Trade like a hedge fund : 20 successful uncorrelated strategies & techniques to winning profits / James Altucher.
        p. cm.
Includes bibliographical references.
    ISBN 0-471-48485-7 (CLOTH)
    1. Stocks. 2. Hedging (Finance) 3. Hedge funds. 4. Speculation. 5. Index mutual funds. 6. Stock exchanges. 7. Profit. 8. Investments. I. Title.
HG4661 .A58 2004
332.6—dc22

                                                                2003020609

Printed in the United States of America

10 9 8 7 6 5

To my father, Seymour Altucher, who taught me

Acknowledgments

This book could not have been completed without the guidance and support of Victor Niederhoffer. *Practical Speculation*, by Victor Niederhoffer and Laurel Kenner, is a must-read.

Thanks to Jim Cramer, for answering my 5,000 e-mails and bringing me on board as a writer for TheStreet.com. Thanks also to Dave Morrow, the editor-in-chief of TheStreet, for not telling Jim to go to hell when he suggested me. The great community among the writers is a tribute to the leadership of Dave and Jim.

Susan Lakatos, the editor at Street Insight has been a *huge* help in editing both my writing on Street Insight as well as many of the techniques in this book. George Moriarty and Gretchen Lembach at The Street have also provided valuable guidance and editing. Many of the writers on Street Insight provided valuable insight and conversations during this process. Particular thanks to Worth Gibson for not only cheering me up on down days, but also placing that bet on Funny Cide for me during the Kentucky Derby.

Dan Kelly, my business partner over the past several years has been an incredible steady rock through the swings that this business often entails. Every system in this book has undergone trial by fire with Dan's and my personal money. Thanks also to Michael Angeledes, Jim Moore, and John Clifford for providing support and advice over this past year.

Dion Kurczek wrote the software, Wealth-Lab, that allowed me to test most of the systems in this book.

Thanks to Pamela van Giessen, my editor at Wiley, for quite possibly being the smartest person in the world, and Lara Murphy at Wiley for helping guide this baby through its final stages.

Finally, thanks to Anne, Josie, and Mollie for providing the sweet and the spice on the days that were particularly sour.

Contents

Introduction

When I first told my investors and partners I was doing a book, most of them were somewhat upset. One of my investors, a prominent hedge fund manager in his own right, was very upset at the thought of sharing good research with people. One of my partners, after reading a few of the sample techniques, told me he was going to buy all of the books when they came out and hold a big bonfire. And then there is always the question I wonder when I read investment books: If these systems are so good, why not just use them to print money all day long? Why write about them?

Well, I have several answers. For one thing, I have learned a lot during the process of researching this book. Although I have been using many of these systems for years, there are always new subtleties, new twists, in every system. Despite being a systematic trader, I am a personal believer that it is impossible to just rest on your laurels and use a black box that prints money forever. Every system needs to be constantly researched and further developed, new avenues explored, former old paths disbanded. Many of the new twists I have looked at during the process of putting together this book actually helped make me money over the past several months—money I perhaps would not have made for myself and my investors if the research had not been so focused. System development and trading is a constantly evolving process. It is that process of continual development that makes someone a successful systematic trader, not the systems themselves.

For another thing, while I believe the systems and patterns mentioned in this book will bring success to those who apply them with discipline, I also feel they should be viewed as stepping stones for further research. The markets are a very big place with many hidden pockets of inefficiency. And yet those pockets are constantly changing. I think the ideas in this book are great places to start when looking for further inefficiencies, and I think the ultimate success readers will enjoy is when they start finding those inefficiencies for themselves.

In addition, I like to correspond with an interested community of other developers, traders, and researchers. Unlike many people I do not believe that the sharing of systems (in most cases) degrades the system. Every year trillions of dollars are put to work in the markets. There are trend followers, countertrend followers, buy and hold mutual funds, day traders trading off gut, and thousands of other types of traders and system followers out there. No matter what system you have or approach you use, it is a guarantee that there is someone out there more than happy to fill your trade in general. By sharing ideas with a community of interested parties, I hope to learn from their ideas as well. The saying, "give and you shall receive" certainly applies here.

Finally, I like to write. I hope people enjoy reading what I write.

In terms of how I would use the ideas in this book: No one system is a Holy Grail for the markets, in the same way that no investor should bet on one stock to blaze his or her way to riches. Just like the buy and hold stock investor, the hedge fund trader relies on diversification, only it is diversification of uncorrelated systems, rather than diversification of uncorrelated stocks. Having a portfolio of systems whose successes do not depend on the successes of other systems is the best way to smooth out any volatility in your personal equity.

Almost all of the systems used in this book were built on top of a simulation software package called Wealth Lab. I cannot recommend this package enough to people. The software can be found at www.wealth-lab.com and comes equipped with a Pascal-like language for building very sophisticated trading systems that can be tested easily on indexes as well as baskets of stocks. The support desk responds quickly to any queries, and the community of developers that can be found on the discussion of forums at the Web site is a useful starting point when developing one's own systems.

One thing to keep in mind is that although testing and research in the markets requires a scientific approach, there is an element that is art as well as science. In other words, do not believe everything you see. Just because something works 500 times out of 500 times does not mean that the developer has not curve fit a system to the data. With every system you ever play, try to ask: Why does this system work? What aspect of the psychology of mob behavior can possibly produce this result?

The markets can only be exploited when there are inefficiencies. That said, there are a lot of smart people trying to find those inefficiencies, and when they occur, they just as often quickly disappear. The inefficiencies that are exploitable, year in and year out, and even decade after decade, are those that have deep roots in the fears and greeds that drive investors and gamblers alike to the world's markets. Keeping this fact in mind will help you avoid the perils of data mining and curve fitting, and will ultimately lead to your own ideas that can be used to trade the markets.

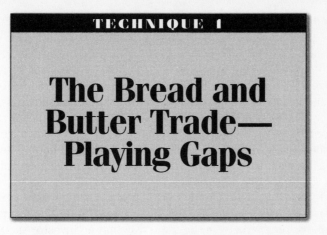

The Bread and Butter Trade— Playing Gaps

The gap trade is the bread and butter trade for many day traders and hedge funds. Many day traders *only* play gaps. They wander into the day trading firm at 9:25 AM, coffee and *New York Post* in hand, settle down, look for the stocks that are gapping up or down, and then fade them. They go the opposite direction: shorting gap ups until they get back to flat with the prior day's close, or going long gap downs. Four times out of five they make money and life is great; they can spend the rest of the day at the movies. But the fifth trade will wipe out all the profits and then some when the gap continues in the direction it started and all the gap-fillers get squeezed in one direction or other.

Research and the systems described in this technique will help the hit rate of the gap filler. The key is to identify those situations where it is more probable than normal that the gap is actually fadable. Making sure in each instance that, through testing and a commitment to research, you know that your edge is real and quantifiable off of all these day-trading wannabes is a key to success in playing gaps.

A gap occurs when a stock opens lower or higher than the previous close. For instance, on October 10, 2001, QLGC closed at 27.98. The stock opened the next day at 29.45 and kept running until it closed at 34.24. In other words, it never "filled the gap," or moved back to the close the day before. Shorting that open would have resulted in a disastrous 17 percent loss that day. (See Figure 1.1)

Note: All example trades are simulated with $100,000 unless otherwise specified.

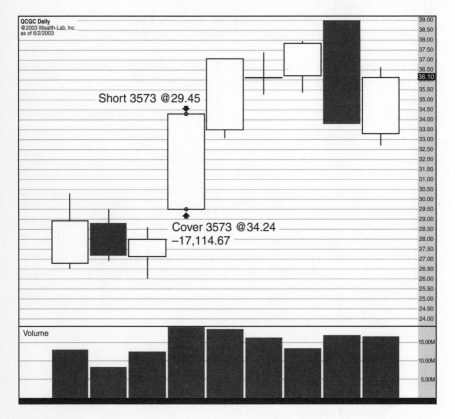

FIGURE 1.1   QLGC on October 10, 2001.

Before deciding to play gaps, first ask the question, "do gaps fill in general?" and then see if one or more trading strategies can develop out of the answer.

SYSTEM #1: FILLING THE GAP

The following is a test of the basic gap-fill approach:

- Buy a stock when it opens more than 2 percent lower than the prior close.
- Sell at yesterday's closing price *or* at the close if yesterday's closing price is never hit.

Test All Nasdaq 100 stocks (including deletions), from January 1, 1999, to June 30, 2003.

Result See Table 1.1. This is not a bad result, but it is not something I would want to play either. While 0.58 percent is a great result per trade if you are dealing with Nasdaq or S&P futures, it is only barely adequate when dealing with individual stocks where commissions and slippage have more of an effect.

This system gets a modest boost if the day before is down, possibly because short-sellers would already be modestly in the money and then the gap gives them an additional profit that they might, at that point, want to take.

TABLE 1.1 Filling the Gap

	All Trades
All Trades	9,821
Average Profit/Loss %	0.58%
Average Bars Held	1
Winning Trades	6,174 (62.87%)
Average Profit %	3.21%
Maximum Consecutive Winning Trades	58
Losing Trades	3,647 (37.13%)
Average Loss %	−3.97%
Maximum Consecutive Losing Trades	20

SYSTEM #2: FILLING THE GAP AFTER DOWN DAY

The rules for System #2 are the same as for System #1 except only buy when not only is there a 2 percent gap down or greater, but also when the day before was a down day for the stock.

Result See Table 1.2. The improvement is decent. The average return per trade goes from 0.58 percent to 0.75 percent. While across 5,000 trades an increase in the average return per trade generates a significant return, it is still not enough per trade if you take into account commissions and slippage, which could be as high as 0.40 percent per trade or more.

A 2 percent gap down does not give us as much to work with as a 5 percent gap down, so let us try a third approach.

TABLE 1.2 Filling Gap after Down Day

	All Trades
All Trades	4,938
Average Profit/Loss %	0.75%
Average Bars Held	1
Winning Trades	3,157 (63.93%)
Average Profit %	3.40%
Average Bars Held	1
Maximum Consecutive Winning Trades	44
Losing Trades	1,781 (36.07%)
Average Loss %	−4.04%
Average Bars Held	0.98
Maximum Consecutive Losing Trades	15

SYSTEM #3: THE 5 PERCENT GAP

- Buy a stock if the stock was down the day before and if the stock is opening 5 percent lower than the close the day before.
- Sell either if the stock hits the close the day before or the stock closes without hitting the profit target.

Result See Table 1.3.

We are finally getting to the point where we might have a system to play. We need to make one more tweak before we arrive at a significantly

TABLE 1.3 5% Gap	
	All Trades
All Trades	993
Average Profit/Loss %	1.97%
Average Bars Held	1
Winning Trades	605 (60.93%)
Average Profit %	6.02%
Average Bars Held	1
Maximum Consecutive Winning Trades	18
Losing Trades	388 (39.07%)
Average Loss %	−4.47%
Average Bars Held	0.97
Maximum Consecutive Losing Trades	10

profitable trading system. So far, gaps get filled more often than not on average, and the results are slightly better when things are even worse (the day before is down and the gap is 5 percent instead of 2 percent). What happens when the market as a whole is gapping down?

SYSTEM #4: THE 5 PERCENT GAP WITH MARKET GAP

- Buy a stock if the stock was down the day before, if the stock is opening 5 percent lower than the close the day before, and if QQQ is also gapping down at least one-half percent.
- Sell if the gap is filled or at the end of the day.

Example: RFMD, 6/26/02

On June 26, 2002, the market had a double-header. Intel had warned on earnings the night before of and on the morning of June 26, consumer confidence numbers came in well below expectations. Basically June 26 was in the middle of a death spiral that culminated in a major low for the market on July 24, 2002. That said, the market backlashed at least for the day on June 26 and buying gap downs produced great profits to the buyers as shown in Figure 1.2. The June 26 bar is in the center of the daily chart in Figure 1.2. After a down June 25, which closed at 25.46, June 26 opened 24.43, almost 4 percent down from the close the day before.

RFMD (in Figure 1.3) closed on June 25 at 6.44 and opened the next morning at 5.70—a disastrous result for those longs who might have felt

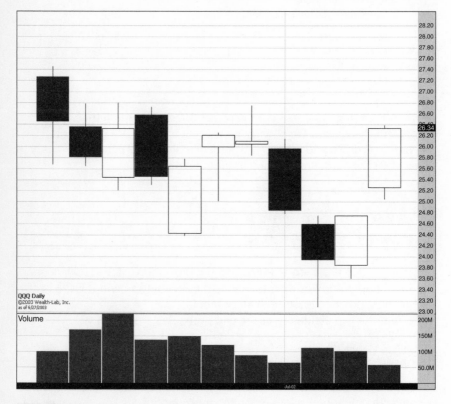

FIGURE 1.2   QQQ on June 26, 2002.

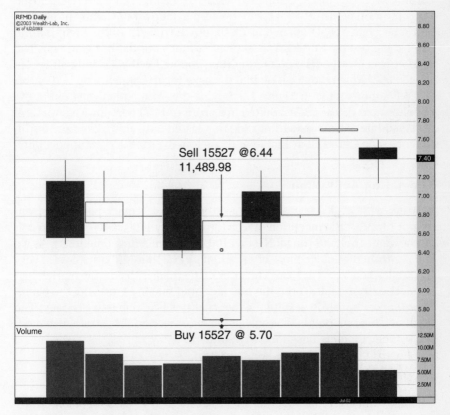

FIGURE 1.3   RFMD on June 26, 2002.

that the world was ending and the worst was yet to come. However, buying that open and selling when RFMD hits the price it had closed at the day before (i.e., it fills the gap), 6.44 would have resulted in a 12.98 percent profit.

Example: YHOO, 7/11/02

On July 11, 2002, the QQQs opened at 23.76 (see Figure 1.4). Having closed the afternoon before at 23.90, which was a gap down of slightly more than half a percent. YHOO opened at 11.15, down from 12.19 the night before. After the close on July 10, Yahoo beat earnings but did not guide up. The market was clearly disappointed in this, hoping for the second-half recovery in 2002, which did not look like it was going to happen.

As demonstrated in Figure 1.5, buying the open and closing out at the open the next day at 12.79 resulted in a profit of 14.71 percent. This was still in the middle of a steep market slide that lasted until July 24, but profits on the long side were still available to those looking for the right opportunity.

Simulation of 5% Gap

Starting with $1,000,000 and using 10 percent of equity per trade from March 10, 1999 (the inception of QQQ) to January 1, 2003, we get the result as shown in Table 1.4 (on all Nasdaq 100 stocks including deletions). As we can see from the equity curve of the simulation (Figure 1.6), there were very few trades generated in 1999. The interesting thing is that as the market had its most extreme falls (note the buy and hold line in Figure 1.6, the equity curve spikes upwards despite the fact that this is a long only strategy. The myth of a bear market is that only going short works. This strategy demonstrates the complete falsehood of that myth.

Figure 1.7 illustrates the annual return.

Average annual return of 28.32 percent with a Sharpe ratio of 1.29.

Many fund of funds take the view that the way to smooth out volatility of returns during both bull and bear markets is to have a long/short strategy. This way, during bull markets the longs will hopefully outperform the shorts and the market (the presumed alpha of the strategy), and during the bear market the shorts will greatly outperform the long positions. However, this strategy demonstrates it is possible to have a long/long strategy during both bull and bear markets by diversifying the method of going long. As an example, we can take the reverse approach of shorting gaps down and try shorting gap ups, as described in System #5.

TABLE 1.4 Simulation of 5% Gap with Market Gap System

	All Trades
Starting Capital	$1,000,000.00
Ending Capital	$2,593,543.00
Net Profit	$1,593,543.00
Net Profit %	159.35%
Exposure %	5.22%
Risk-Adjusted Return	3053.37%
All Trades	525
Average Profit/Loss	$3,035.32
Average Profit/Loss %	2.07%
Average Bars Held	1
Winning Trades	321 (61.14%)
Gross Profit	$2,875,406.00
Average Profit	$8,957.65
Average Profit %	5.89%
Average Bars Held	1
Maximum Consecutive Winning Trades	13
Losing Trades	204 (38.86%)
Gross Loss	($1,281,862.38)
Average Loss	($6,283.64)
Average Loss %	−4.07%
Average Bars Held	0.97
Maximum Consecutive Losing Trades	14
Maximum Drawdown	−8.26%
Maximum Drawdown $	($168,763.75)
Maximum Drawdown Date	9/6/2001
Recovery Factor	9.44
Profit Factor	2.24
Payoff Ratio	1.44
Risk Reward Ratio	3.37
Sharpe Ratio of Trades	6.59

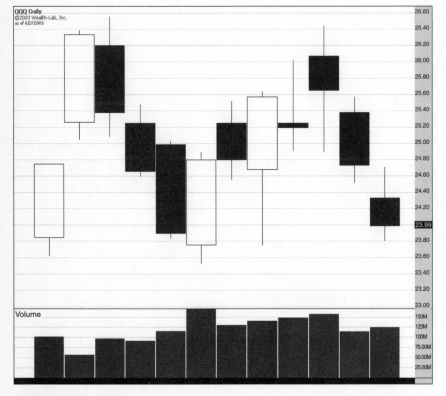

FIGURE 1.4   QQQs on July 11, 2002.

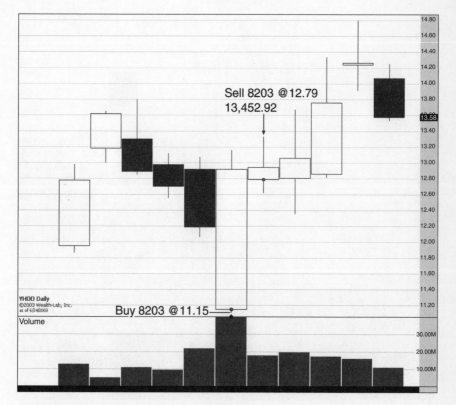

FIGURE 1.5   YHOO on July 11, 2002.

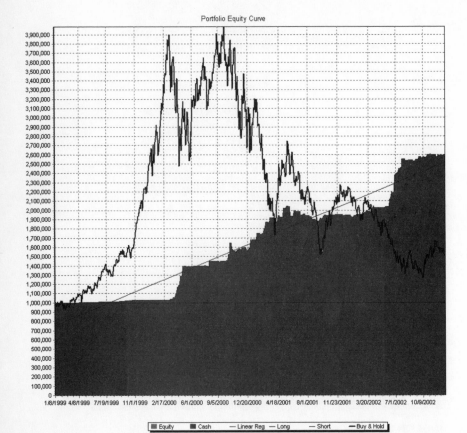

FIGURE 1.6   Portfolio equity curve.

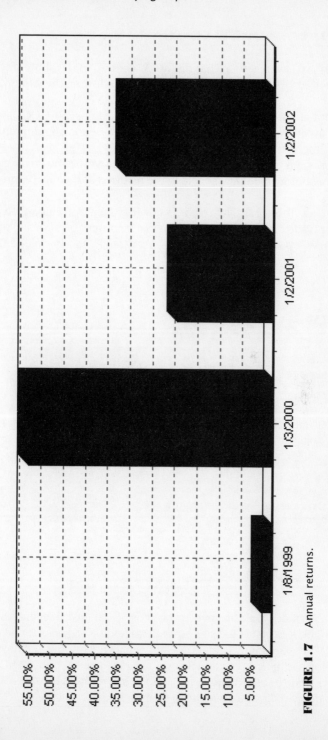

FIGURE 1.7 Annual returns.

SYSTEM #5: SHORTING THE GAP UP

Previously we saw a gap up that did not work out on the short side: QLGC on October 10, 2001. Here are the rules for the shorting the gap up system:

- Short a stock when the stock is up the day before, the QQQs are gapping up at least one-half percent, and the stock is gapping up greater than 5 percent.
- Cover when the stock closes the gap (i.e., cover at the closing price of the day before); otherwise, close the position at the day before.

Result See Table 1.5. The result is not that great, producing an average return per trade of –0.56 percent. Even in a bear market, shorting too much exuberance (sometimes referred to as "irrational") has not paid off for the speculator.

TABLE 1.5 Short Trades

All Trades	752
Average Profit/Loss %	–0.56%
Average Bars Held	1
Winning Trades	371 (49.34%)
Average Profit %	4.15%
Average Bars Held	1
Maximum Consecutive Winning Trades	16
Losing Trades	381 (50.66%)
Average Loss %	–5.20%
Average Bars Held	0.99
Maximum Consecutive Losing Trades	16

SYSTEM #6: SWING TRADING THE GAP

The gap-fill trades do not have to be closed out just because the gap is filled. In fact, it is better to hold on to them and try to press for as much as possible. There are many trade-offs between swing trading and day trading. Holding for multiple days allows you to reduce transaction costs and also allows the trade to take advantage of gap ups overnight. However, the night contains many risks and being in cash allows one to sleep easy.

It can be seen that taking System #4 and adding a simple step that allows us to hold overnight drastically increases the profitability of the system, which becomes System #6 with the following rules:

- Buy a stock when the stock is down the day before, QQQ is gapping down more than half a percent, and the stock is gapping down more than 5 percent.
- Hold the stock at least until the next morning.
- Sell when the stock goes lower than the prior day's close.

Example: CIEN, 4/17/01

CIEN closed at 51.51 on April 16, 2001 (Figure 1.8). The next day it gapped down to 48.11 before reversing and closing at 53.09. The stock then gapped up on April 18 and kept going for two more days before finally stalling on April 20. Since it opened that day lower than the close the day before at 67.30, the trade was stopped out at the open at 67.09 for a 38.22 percent profit.

Simulation

See Table 1.6. While there were not that many trades in 1999, we can see that from 2000 to 2002, the worse the market did, the better the equity curve of the swing trade gap system (Figure 1.9, page 18).

Drawdown Analysis   The drawdown (Figure 1.10, page 19) is relatively mild except in April, 2000, the end of 2000 (right before the first rate cut), and the week immediately following September 11, 2001.

Equity High Analysis   In every case except two, it took fewer than three months to achieve a new equity high in the system. In the two exceptions, it took a maximum of five months to achieve the new equity high. (See Figure 1.11, page 20.)

Annual Return of Simulation   Gaps create enormous anxiety for the average investor. When a stock gaps down because of an earnings warning, for instance, the first reaction often is to panic. Thus, even before the open, investors are trying to sell in a panic, causing the gap even before the news is properly disseminated and analyzed. This type of behavior is more often than not going to be irrational behavior and can be, over the long run, exploited profitably. (See Figure 1.12, page 21.)

FIGURE 1.8   CIEN on April 17, 2001.

TABLE 1.6 Simulation of Swing Trading the Gap

	All Trades
Starting Capital	$1,000,000.00
Ending Capital	$4,726,416.00
Net Profit	$3,726,416.00
Net Profit %	372.64%
Exposure %	5.68%
Risk-Adjusted Return	6560.19%
All Trades	498
Average Profit/Loss	$7,482.76
Average Profit/Loss %	3.64%
Average Bars Held	1.24
Winning Trades	300 (60.24%)
Gross Profit	$6,028,952.00
Average Profit	$20,096.51
Average Profit %	9.41%
Average Bars Held	1.37
Maximum Consecutive Winning Trades	24
Losing Trades	198 (39.76%)
Gross Loss	($2,302,538.00)
Average Loss	($11,628.98)
Average Loss %	−5.26%
Average Bars Held	1.02
Maximum Consecutive Losing Trades	14
Maximum Drawdown	−11.89%
Maximum Drawdown $	($289,220.50)
Maximum Drawdown Date	11/13/2000
Recovery Factor	12.88
Profit Factor	2.62
Payoff Ratio	1.79
Standard Error	$452,060.94
Risk Reward Ratio	1.81
Sharpe Ratio of Trades	5

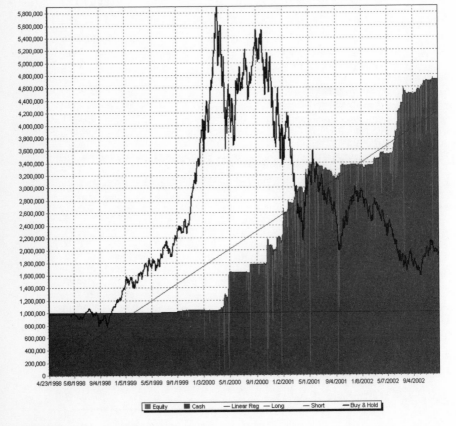

FIGURE 1.9   Portfolio equity curve.

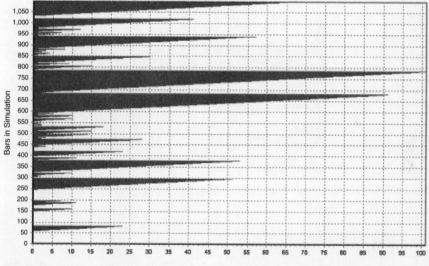

FIGURE 1.10 Drawdown analysis.

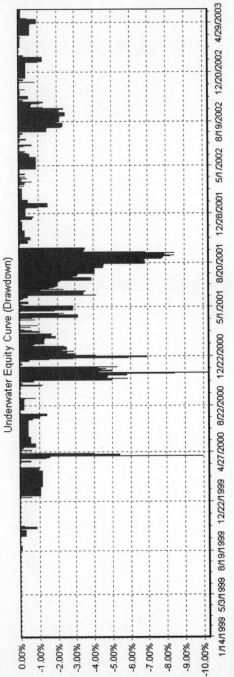

FIGURE 1.11   Underwater equity curve.

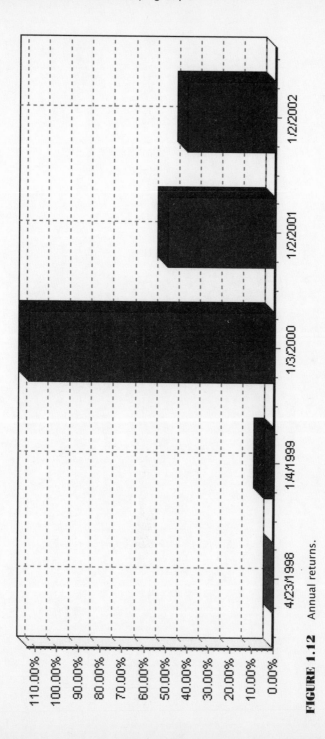

FIGURE 1.12   Annual returns.

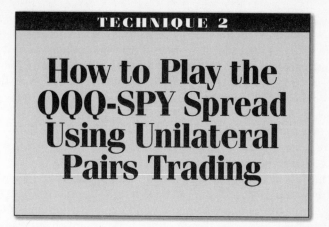

How to Play the QQQ-SPY Spread Using Unilateral Pairs Trading

At first glance unilateral pairs trading seems like a contradiction in terms. *Pairs trading* usually implies a market neutral strategy where you go long one asset and short another asset. *Unilateral* means we are going to take just one side of the pair. Many hedge funds use a pairs trading strategy and we discuss one such strategy in Technique 15 on preferred stock arbitrage. While pairs trading at first glance seems safer than *directional* trading where one takes a bias in the market, up or down, and bets on that bias, the reality is that often pairs trading can be much less safe than other forms of trading. A common slogan used to refer to this pairs trading is: "Twice the risk and half the gain," and that's largely true.

When you trade a pair, although you are usually neutral on the market, you are, in fact, making a very biased bet on the direction of the spread between those two asset classes. As an example, say GM and F normally trade in lockstep with each other, but then F suddenly moves down sharply without GM moving down sharply. One might short GM and go long F with the idea that the spread between the two stocks goes back to its historical norm. In other words, we are betting on a mean reversion of the spread.

The preferred stock arbitrage strategy we discuss is different from normal pairs trading strategies in that the key to the success of the convertible arbitrage strategy is not that we were betting on the direction of the spread but, rather, on getting an exorbitant yield. If the spread went in our direction that would be great, otherwise, no big deal (although we would not want it to go too much against us).

Pairs trading often involves heavy doses of leverage because spreads of highly correlated assets might only need to get a tiny bit out of whack to make the trade worthwhile. Leverage in these situations is where many hedge funds get in trouble. In 99 times out of 100, the spread might get back in shape, but if just one or two get way out of line, then that could be the difference between a 20 percent return on the year and a –50 percent return on the year.

The other problem with pairs trading in general is that there are many billions of dollars in hedge funds doing a variety of pairs trading strategies, merger arbitrage being the most common pairs trading strategy. If Company A is buying Company B in stock, then suddenly those two assets should trade in perfect lockstep with each other, and as the deal date gets close, the price of Company B should converge on the price that Company A is paying for it. Because the amount of money involved in playing the merger arbitrage strategy is so great, the only way to really lock in a good return in most cases (particularly when the deal is extremely likely to close) is to use leverage. If the deal falls through at the last minute, as occasionally happens, look out below.

There are other types of pairs trading strategies, for instance, going long a basket of low P/E stocks in a sector and short high P/E stocks in the same sector. Going long and short same duration bonds that expire on different dates (the closer the date, the more likely it is to be accurately priced, whereas the further out bond might be mispriced). The most common type of pairs trading strategy, which we focus on in this technique, is when the ratio (spread) between two assets that are highly correlated moves out of kilter with its historical norm.

The key difference in using unilateral pairs trading is that we will not trade both sides of the spread, but the side that is historically more volatile. The idea is that the more volatile side is most often the culprit for why the spread has gone awry. For this reason we will treat QQQ and SPY as a pair, but we will only trade QQQ.

THE UNILATERAL PAIRS TRADING SYSTEM FOR QQQ-SPY

1. Calculate the ratio of the QQQ price series over the SPY price series. For example, on May 1, 2003, SPY was 91.92 and QQQ was 27.42. The ratio for that day was 27.42/91.92, or 0.298.
2. Calculate the 20-day moving average of that ratio.

3. For each day, calculate the difference between the ratio and its moving average.

4. Calculate the 20-day moving average of those differences.

5. For each day, calculate how many standard deviations the difference in ratios is for that day from its moving average. Calculate the standard deviation for each day using its prior 20 days.

6. For each day, if the standard deviation calculated is greater than 1.5 *and* QQQ is 2 percent greater than the prior day, then *short* QQQ. (In other words, the spread between QQQ and SPY has become much greater than usual. If this is true and QQQ had a big up move, then QQQ is most likely the culprit and needs to be shorted.)

7. For each day, if the standard deviation calculated is less than –1.5 *and* QQQ is 2 percent lower than the prior day, then *buy* QQQ.

8. *Sell/cover* when the standard deviation of the difference in the ratios is less than 0.5 (in the case of a short) or greater than –0.5 (in the case of a long).

The system is pretty complicated to put together and requires some coding. The code is presented in the Appendix to this technique.

EXAMPLES

QQQ, 5/20/03

On May 19, 2003, QQQ fell almost 3.6 percent and SPY fell 2.3 percent. Sure enough, this was larger than the usual ratio of percent changes between the two exchange traded funds (ETFs), specifically more than 2 standard deviations away from the average difference between the ratio between the two assets and the 20-day moving average of that ratio. In Figure 2.1, the top pane maps out the standard deviations between the ratio for that day and the 20-day moving average of the ratio. In the second pane, the wavy line is the ratio and the straighter line is the 20-day moving average of that ratio.

Since on May 19 QQQ had fallen over 2 percent, the system buys at the open the next day at 27.76 and holds until the number of standard deviations between the ratio and its moving average goes back above –0.5 standard deviations, which occurs on May 28. The system sells at 29.16 for a 5.04 percent profit.

FIGURE 2.1   QQQ on May 20, 2003.

QQQ, 7/8/02

On July 5, 2002, people were relieved that July 4 had come and gone with no terrorist attack. Things were not that simple, though, for everyone who had shorted QQQs in order to hedge their portfolios against the possibility of an attack. Everyone who shorted now had to cover that short and the race was on to see who would cover first. QQQ ended up over 6.4 percent that day and SPY up 3.9 percent. While the SPY rally was very sharp, the QQQ rally was its largest one day move of the year and put the ratio for that day 2 standard deviations above the 20-day moving average for that ratio. (See Figure 2.2, see page 30.)

Shorting at the open on July 8 at 26.20 and then covering when the standard deviation between the ratio and the 20-day moving average of the ratio was back down to 0.5 would have had one cover on July 26 at 22.56 for a 13.89 percent profit.

In the results (Table 2.1) I ran a simulation on QQQ using the unilateral pairs trading system starting with $1M and using 100 percent of equity per trade. I came up with 72 percent success with an average return per trade of 2.72 percent. The magic of compounding allows for a remarkable return of 462 percent over the past four years.

The annual returns were as shown in Figure 2.3 (see page 31) and Table 2.2 (see page 32), for an average annual return of 48 percent. Note that in the incredible bull market year of 1999, the system did not work as well. In 1999 things were basically straight up for tech stocks, with the rest of the market doing much more poorly. Shorting QQQs in those cases did not work as well.

We can see in Figure 2.4 (see page 33) depicting the drawdown analysis that the bulk of the drawdown occurred during the final part of the bull run. In general, though the equity curve of the system for QQQ has been fairly smooth, as shown in Figure 2.5 (see page 34), with most of the profits coming from the long side, but with the short side still holding up its end of the bargain.

TABLE 2.1 Simulation of Unilateral Pairs Using QQQ

	All Trades	Long Trades	Short Trades	Buy & Hold
Starting Capital	$1,000,000.00	$1,000,000.00	$1,000,000.00	$1,000,000.00
Ending Capital	$5,621,253.00	$4,156,423.00	$2,464,831.25	$583,056.63
Net Profit	$4,621,253.00	$3,156,423.00	$1,464,831.25	($416,943.34)
Net Profit %	462.13%	315.64%	146.48%	–41.69%
Exposure %	15.94%	8.80%	9.78%	100.11%
Risk-Adjusted Return	2898.31%	3588.11%	1497.51%	–41.65%
All Trades	72	40	32	1
Average Profit/Loss	$64,184.07	$78,910.58	$45,775.98	($416,943.34)
Average Profit/Loss %	2.72%	3.47%	1.78%	–41.65%
Average Bars Held	5.88	5.25	6.66	4,999.00
Winning Trades	52 (72.22%)	31 (77.50%)	21 (65.63%)	0 (0.00%)
Gross Profit	$6,904,063.00	$3,960,379.50	$2,943,683.50	$0.00
Average Profit	$132,770.44	$127,754.18	$140,175.41	$0.00
Average Profit %	5.59%	5.52%	5.70%	0.00%
Average Bars Held	4.69	4.58	4.86	0
Maximum Consecutive Winning Trades	8	7	6	0

Losing Trades	20 (27.78%)	9 (22.50%)	11 (34.38%)	1 (100.00%)
Gross Loss	($2,282,810.00)	($803,957.25)	($1,478,852.75)	($416,943.34)
Average Loss	($114,140.50)	($89,328.59)	($134,441.16)	($416,943.34)
Average Loss %	-4.74%	-3.59%	-5.69%	-41.65%
Average Bars Held	8.95	7.56	10.09	4,999.00
Maximum Consecutive Losing Trades	3	2	3	1
Maximum Drawdown	-23.12%	-15.11%	-27.85%	-83.00%
Maximum Drawdown $	($806,246.00)	($406,770.50)	($806,246.00)	($1,913,161.00)
Maximum Drawdown Date	11/23/1999	4/4/2001	4/20/2001	10/9/2002
Recovery Factor	5.73	7.76	1.82	0.22
Profit Factor	3.02	4.93	1.99	0
Payoff Ratio	1.18	1.54	1	0
Standard Error	$889,203.00	$585,986.38	$313,635.31	$231,135.34
Risk Reward Ratio	0.12	0.12	0.1	-0.01
Sharpe Ratio of Trades	2.81	4.4	1.48	0

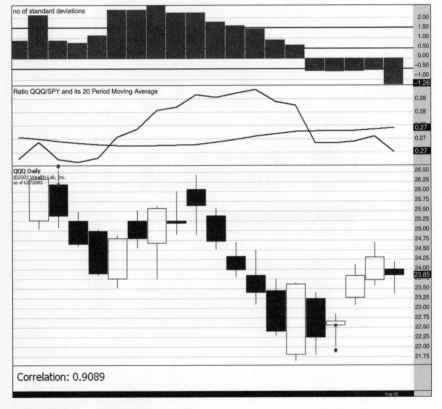

FIGURE 2.2   QQQ on July 8, 2002.

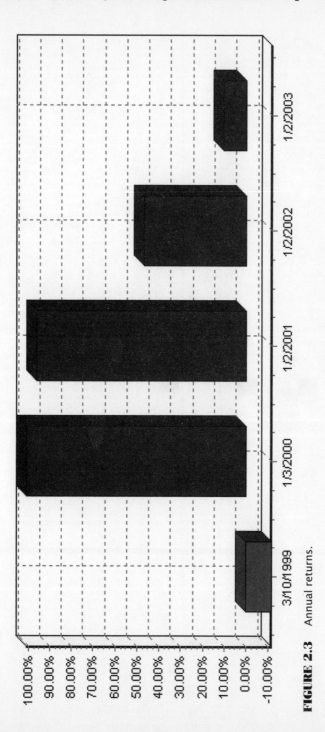

FIGURE 2.3 Annual returns.

TABLE 2.2 Annual Returns

Period Starting	$ Return	% Return	% Max DD	Exposure	Entries	Exits
3/10/1999	−118,052.88	−11.81	−23.12	1.5	10	10
1/3/2000	889,356.63	100.84	−12.85	39.72	20	20
1/2/2001	1,698,867.75	95.91	−19.62	38.42	20	19
1/2/2002	1,626,432.00	46.87	−14.2	41.58	17	18
1/2/2003	524,649.50	10.29	−4.49	26.69	5	5

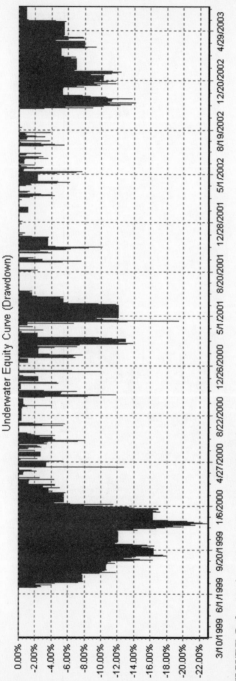

FIGURE 2.4 Underwater equity curve (drawdown).

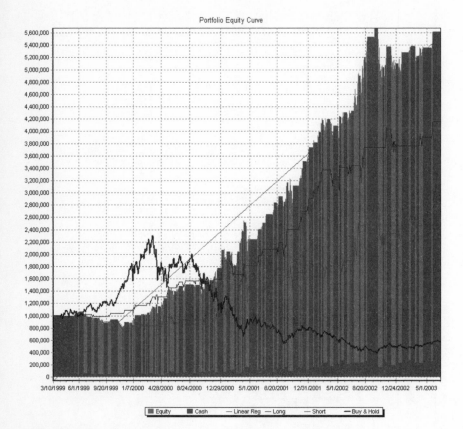

FIGURE 2.5 Portfolio equity curve.

TABLE 2.3   Unilateral Pairs Trading (QQQ/SPY)

Position	Symbol	Shares	Entry Date	Entry Price	Exit Date	Exit Price	% Change	Net Profit	Bars Held	Cum Profit
Short	QQQ	17,126	5/13/1999	55.9	5/14/1999	53.38	4.51	43,157.53	1	43,157.53
Long	QQQ	19,879	5/26/1999	50.5	5/28/1999	51.5	1.98	19,879.00	2	63,036.53
Short	QQQ	18,629	6/17/1999	53.5	7/2/1999	58	-8.41	-83,830.50	11	-20,793.97
Long	QQQ	15,928	7/21/1999	58.53	8/2/1999	56.69	-3.14	-29,307.52	8	-50,101.49
Short	QQQ	15,653	8/16/1999	57.62	9/9/1999	61.56	-6.84	-61,672.86	17	-111,774.35
Long	QQQ	14,063	9/24/1999	59.62	10/8/1999	62.85	5.42	45,423.48	10	-66,350.87
Short	QQQ	13,287	11/4/1999	67.68	11/23/1999	76.44	-12.94	-116,394.15	13	-182,745.02
Short	QQQ	10,025	11/26/1999	78.4	11/30/1999	76.57	2.33	18,345.77	2	-164,399.25
Long	QQQ	10,800	12/1/1999	74.32	12/3/1999	79.32	6.73	54,000.00	2	-110,399.25
Short	QQQ	9,449	12/22/1999	89.19	12/29/1999	90	-0.91	-7,653.67	4	-118,052.91
Short	QQQ	8,842	1/4/2000	92	1/5/2000	87.5	4.89	39,789.00	1	-78,263.91
Long	QQQ	10,181	1/6/2000	86.88	1/11/2000	91.75	5.61	49,581.50	3	-28,682.42
Long	QQQ	10,485	1/12/2000	89	1/18/2000	92.07	3.45	32,188.95	3	3,506.53
Short	QQQ	9,289	2/9/2000	102.07	2/16/2000	99.9	2.13	20,157.11	5	23,663.64
Short	QQQ	9,328	2/24/2000	104.88	2/29/2000	105.75	-0.83	-8,115.39	3	15,548.26
Long	QQQ	9,176	3/3/2000	108	3/6/2000	111.75	3.47	34,410.00	1	49,958.26
Long	QQQ	9,289	3/15/2000	106.5	3/28/2000	116.98	9.84	97,348.75	9	147,307.00
Long	QQQ	10,588	4/4/2000	103.62	4/10/2000	107.62	3.86	42,352.00	4	189,659.00
Long	QQQ	12,284	4/13/2000	92.81	4/18/2000	89.48	-3.59	-40,905.65	3	148,753.34
Short	QQQ	11,959	4/28/2000	93.56	5/11/2000	82.75	11.55	129,276.76	9	278,030.09
Long	QQQ	16,229	5/24/2000	75	5/31/2000	84.47	12.63	153,688.66	4	431,718.75
Short	QQQ	14,528	6/5/2000	92.25	6/23/2000	95	-2.98	-39,952.00	14	391,766.75
Long	QQQ	14,427	6/30/2000	91.81	7/13/2000	97.94	6.68	88,437.58	8	480,204.31
Long	QQQ	15,306	7/28/2000	92.19	8/9/2000	93.69	1.63	22,959.00	8	503,163.31

(continued)

TABLE 2.3 Continued

Position	Symbol	Shares	Entry Date	Entry Price	Exit Date	Exit Price	% Change	Net Profit	Bars Held	Cum Profit
Long	QQQ	15,386	9/12/2000	93.5	9/20/2000	93.37	-0.14	-2,000.14	6	501,163.19
Long	QQQ	16,977	10/4/2000	83.5	10/16/2000	81.12	-2.85	-40,405.21	8	460,757.97
Short	QQQ	16,314	10/20/2000	84.5	10/26/2000	78.19	7.47	102,941.30	4	563,699.25
Long	QQQ	19,623	11/9/2000	74.75	11/16/2000	75.37	0.83	12,166.31	5	575,865.56
Long	QQQ	23,785	11/30/2000	61.75	12/4/2000	64.12	3.84	56,370.52	2	632,236.06
Short	QQQ	21,935	12/6/2000	70.59	12/15/2000	64.25	8.98	139,067.81	7	771,303.88
Long	QQQ	31,488	1/3/2001	52.19	1/4/2001	61.63	18.09	297,246.81	1	1,068,550.75
Short	QQQ	31,726	1/12/2001	62.75	1/26/2001	63.56	-1.29	-25,698.10	9	1,042,852.63
Long	QQQ	33,010	2/9/2001	58.25	2/27/2001	51.54	-11.52	-221,497.06	11	821,355.56
Short	QQQ	35,026	3/7/2001	50.4	3/12/2001	44	12.7	224,166.45	3	1,045,522.00
Short	QQQ	44,920	3/20/2001	43.44	3/21/2001	40.52	6.72	131,166.31	1	1,176,688.25
Short	QQQ	48,314	3/23/2001	43.55	3/29/2001	39.38	9.58	201,469.30	4	1,378,157.50
Long	QQQ	65,183	4/4/2001	34.71	4/6/2001	36.9	6.31	142,750.92	2	1,520,908.38
Short	QQQ	58,411	4/12/2001	40.3	4/27/2001	45.15	-12.03	-283,293.47	10	1,237,614.88
Long	QQQ	47,844	5/31/2001	44.54	6/6/2001	48.08	7.95	169,367.80	4	1,406,982.63
Long	QQQ	54,121	6/15/2001	41.8	6/22/2001	43.62	4.35	98,500.20	5	1,505,482.88
Short	QQQ	52,083	7/2/2001	45.65	7/6/2001	43.01	5.78	137,499.28	3	1,642,982.13
Short	QQQ	58,255	8/2/2001	43.79	8/9/2001	40.41	7.72	196,901.97	5	1,839,884.13
Long	QQQ	71,448	8/20/2001	37.85	8/27/2001	39.28	3.78	102,170.66	5	1,942,054.75
Long	QQQ	91,637	9/19/2001	30.64	9/25/2001	29.71	-3.04	-85,222.44	4	1,856,832.25
Long	QQQ	94,663	9/27/2001	28.4	10/4/2001	31.65	11.44	307,654.75	5	2,164,487.00
Short	QQQ	92,500	10/11/2001	33.19	10/30/2001	33.71	-1.57	-48,100.04	13	2,116,387.00
Short	QQQ	76,658	11/21/2001	38.47	11/27/2001	40.05	4.11	121,119.48	3	2,237,506.50
Long	QQQ	79,371	11/29/2001	39.03	12/5/2001	41.2	5.56	172,235.23	4	2,409,741.75

Short	QQQ	75,595	12/6/2001	42.7	12/10/2001	41.32	3.23	104,321.18	2	2,514,063.00
Long	QQQ	86,062	12/21/2001	39.42	1/4/2002	41.95	6.42	217,737.08	8	2,731,800.00
Long	QQQ	94,791	1/23/2002	37.65	1/25/2002	38.47	2.18	77,728.59	2	2,809,528.50
Long	QQQ	102,843	2/8/2002	35.46	2/14/2002	37.15	4.77	173,804.92	4	2,983,333.50
Long	QQQ	113,027	2/22/2002	33.61	2/27/2002	35.39	5.3	201,187.92	3	3,184,521.50
Short	QQQ	107,006	3/5/2002	36.93	3/20/2002	36.87	0.16	6,420.51	11	3,190,942.00
Long	QQQ	113,462	4/3/2002	35.3	4/16/2002	34.43	-2.46	-98,711.82	9	3,092,230.25
Long	QQQ	127,421	5/3/2002	30.47	5/9/2002	31.57	3.61	140,163.16	4	3,232,393.50
Short	QQQ	123,450	5/15/2002	32.08	5/28/2002	31.47	1.9	75,304.81	8	3,307,698.25
Long	QQQ	144,604	6/10/2002	28.36	6/18/2002	28.31	-0.18	-7,230.37	6	3,300,468.00
Long	QQQ	154,400	6/21/2002	26.36	6/25/2002	26.58	0.83	33,967.89	2	3,334,436.00
Short	QQQ	156,329	7/8/2002	26.2	7/26/2002	22.56	13.89	569,037.75	14	3,903,473.75
Long	QQQ	204,940	8/2/2002	22.78	8/15/2002	24.24	6.41	299,212.22	9	4,202,686.00
Short	QQQ	191,943	8/22/2002	25.74	8/28/2002	24.02	6.68	330,141.84	4	4,532,828.00
Short	QQQ	240,337	9/26/2002	22.16	9/27/2002	21.55	2.75	146,605.72	1	4,679,433.50
Short	QQQ	255,951	10/11/2002	21.55	10/30/2002	24.06	-11.65	-642,437.06	13	4,036,996.50
Short	QQQ	184,754	11/5/2002	25.71	11/8/2002	25.49	0.86	40,645.75	3	4,077,642.25
Long	QQQ	198,426	11/12/2002	24.4	11/15/2002	25.9	6.15	297,639.00	3	4,375,281.00
Long	QQQ	192,191	12/5/2002	26.95	12/24/2002	25.5	-5.38	-278,677.09	13	4,096,604.00
Short	QQQ	183,957	1/7/2003	26.41	1/21/2003	25.41	3.79	183,957.00	9	4,280,561.00
Short	QQQ	198,674	2/19/2003	25.2	2/26/2003	24.68	2.06	103,310.57	5	4,383,871.50
Short	QQQ	199,636	3/14/2003	25.73	3/20/2003	26.54	-3.15	-161,705.44	4	4,222,166.00
Long	QQQ	196,477	4/1/2003	25.44	4/17/2003	26.16	2.83	141,463.31	12	4,363,629.50
Long	QQQ	184,017	5/20/2003	27.76	5/28/2003	29.16	5.04	257,623.73	5	4,621,253.00

SMH and QQQ, 3/5/02

This system will work on any two assets that are highly correlated where one asset is more volatile than the other. For instance, SMH, which is the ETF tracking the semiconductor sector, is correlated with QQQ (all of the components of SMH are also components of QQQ) and has been more volatile since its inception on June 5, 2000. Using QQQ as the other member of the pair but trading SMH according to the rules previously described would have the results shown in Table 2.4.

The market in general had been selling off pretty harshly in the latter half of February 2002, the chip stocks most of all. After the Nasdaq had failed to hold onto the 2000 level in January and with "Enron-itis" starting to creep into the market in the various incarnations of TYC and WCOM, investors got cold feet and decided to bail. SMH had several 2 percent down days in a row before getting out of whack with its QQQ counterpart, triggering a buy signal on the morning of March 1 at 40.77. The market as a whole rebounded the first week of March, with the chip stocks leading the pack. The spread between SMH and QQQ got back down to normal levels (i.e., less than 0.5 standard deviations away from the average spread) on March 5 when the system sold at 46.85 for a 14.91 percent profit (Figure 2.6).

TABLE 2.4 Results

	All Trades	Long Trades	Short Trades	Buy & Hold
All Trades	38	19	19	1
Average Profit/Loss %	3.90%	2.24%	5.56%	−71.22%
Average Bars Held	6.74	6.21	7.26	767
Winning Trades	26 (68.42%)	11 (57.89%)	15 (78.95%)	0
Average Profit %	7.44%	6.47%	8.15%	0.00%
Average Bars Held	5.62	4.27	6.6	0
Maximum Consecutive Winning Trades	6	3	6	0
Losing Trades	12 (31.58%)	8 (42.11%)	4 (21.05%)	1
Average Loss %	−3.76%	−3.56%	−4.16%	−71.22%
Average Bars Held	9.17	8.88	9.75	767
Maximum Consecutive Losing Trades	2	2	1	1

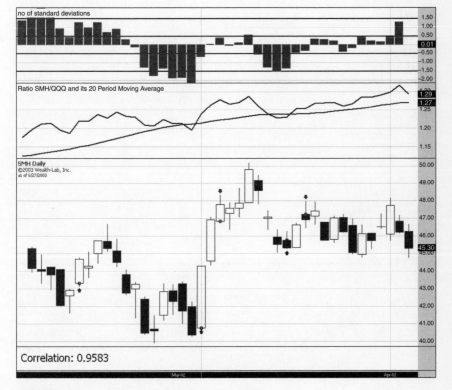

FIGURE 2.6   SMH and QQQ on March 5, 2002.

KLAC, 4/10/01

This technique can also be used to play the spread between stocks and their peers. For instance, KLAC and NVLS are the two top components of the Philadelphia Semiconductor Index (the "SOX"), making up 12 percent and 9 percent of the index, respectively. Viewing KLAC and NVLS as a pair but trading KLAC according to the rules previously specified has the results shown in Table 2.5.

TABLE 2.5   Results

	All Trades	Long Trades	Short Trades
All Trades	57	25	32
Average Profit/Loss %	2.84%	5.99%	0.37%
Average Bars Held	6.47	7.04	6.03
Winning Trades	33 (57.89%)	16 (64.00%)	17 (53.13%)
Gross Profit	$325,058.03	$194,534.89	$130,523.16
Average Bars Held	5.52	6.44	4.65
Maximum Consecutive			
Winning Trades	10	8	5
Losing Trades	24 (42.11%)	9 (36.00%)	15 (46.88%)
Average Loss %	−6.75%	−4.96%	−7.82%
Average Bars Held	7.79	8.11	7.6
Maximum Consecutive			
Losing Trades	6	2	5

In the week prior to April 10, 2001, KLAC fell over 25 percent and NVLS (shown in the third panel of Figure 2.7) fell about 20%. Consequently, the average spread between these two highly correlated stocks fell about 2 standard deviations from its norm. Meanwhile, KLAC had a greater than 2 percent down day on April 9, so all of the conditions were in place. Buying KLAC on April 10 at 34.45 and holding until the standard deviation of the spread fell back below 0.5 standard deviations would have resulted in a profit of 54.28 percent when the system sold on April 20 at 53.15.

ALTR, 7/17/2000

Semiconductor equipment makers ALTR and XLNX make another good pair of highly correlated stocks, with ALTR being the more volatile of the two. In fact, no other components of the Nasdaq 100 are as highly correlated. Using these two as the pair and ALTR as the trading vehicle we get the result shown in Table 2.6 (see page 42).

FIGURE 2.7   KLAC on April 10, 2001.

TABLE 2.6 Results

	All Trades	Long Trades	Short Trades
All Trades	56	30	26
Average Profit/Loss %	4.09%	5.06%	2.97%
Average Bars Held	7.3	6.4	8.35
Winning Trades	39 (69.64%)	21 (70.00%)	18 (69.23%)
Average Profit %	9.88%	10.41%	9.26%
Average Bars Held	7.44	6.86	8.11
Maximum Consecutive Winning Trades	6	5	7
Losing Trades	17 (30.36%)	9 (30.00%)	8 (30.77%)
Average Loss %	−9.18%	−7.41%	−11.17%
Average Bars Held	7	5.33	8.88
Maximum Consecutive Losing Trades	3	1	3

In the week before July 17, 2000, ALTR went up over 20 percent, with XLNX only following about 12 percent. Consequently the ratio between the two assets was about 2 standard deviations higher than the moving average of the ratio. After ALTR then had a big up day (but down open to close, interestingly), the system shorted ALTR at the open the next day at 59.22. The ratio did not get back to historic norms for eight days, finally settling down on July 27, when the system covered ALTR at 48.47 for an 18.15 percent profit. (See Figure 2.8.)

CONCLUSION

With more than 10,000 stocks and many other asset classes—commodities, foreign stocks, indices, bonds, and so on—there are more than enough opportunities to find highly correlated pairs and map out the spreads between those pairs. Many books have been written about common arbitrage and pairs trading techniques. Books on merger arbitrage, relative value arbitrage, capital structure arbitrage, and convertible arbitrage are lining the shelves of your local bookstore. However, my personal feeling is that all of these strategies are too crowded and it is getting harder to make money on the small spreads that the strategies covered in these books try to exploit.

By mapping out the correlations between very liquid and highly correlated instruments such as QQQ and SPY, SMH and QQQ, KLAC and NVLS, and so on, you can find opportunities that will arise in the spreads between these assets, regardless of market direction.

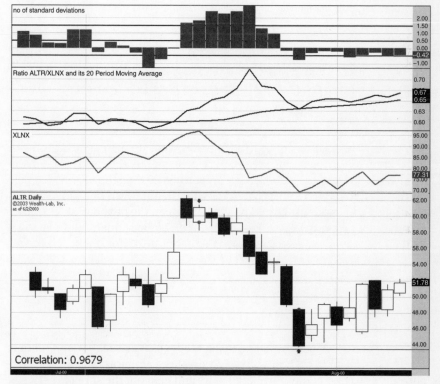

FIGURE 2.8 ALTR on July 17, 2000.

APPENDIX

Unilateral Pairs Trading Code

```
VAR Close1, Close2, RatioPane, StDevPane, TextPane, Bar, Sym, ActualRatioSeries,
  ActualRatioSMASeries, DeltaSeries, DeltaSMASeries,
  DeltaDifferenceSeries, DeltaNormSeries, MAPeriod: Integer;
VAR Up_Threshold, Down_Threshold, Exit_Up_Threshold, Exit_Down_Threshold,
  R, Value, atr1, atr2: float;
VAR Stock1, Stock2, LongSymbol, ShortSymbol, CurrentSymbol, TestSymbol: STRING;
// assigning values to variables
Up_Threshold := 1.5;
Down_Threshold := -1.5;
Exit_Up_Threshold := 0.5; // positions entered above Up_Threshold are exited here
Exit_Down_Threshold := -0.5; // positions entered below Down_Threshold are exited
here
//MAPeriod := #OptVar3;
MAPeriod := 20;
// If you want to enter your symbols manually, comment the code between the ****
// out and enter your stocks in the lines between the ####, then click on one of
// the stocks of the chosen pair in your watchlist
// ****************************************************************************
// This loop makes sure all series are synchronized
FOR SYM := 0 TO WatchListCount - 1 DO
 SetPrimarySeries( WatchListSymbol( SYM));
// end of synch loop
// find the best correlated symbol
R := 0.0;
LongSymbol := '';
Value := -1.0;
CurrentSymbol := GetSymbol;
FOR SYM := 0 TO WatchListCount - 1 DO
BEGIN
 TestSymbol := WatchListSymbol( SYM);
 SetPrimarySeries(TestSymbol);
 Close1 := #Close;
 RestorePrimarySeries;
 R := Correlation( Close1, #Close, 0, BarCount - 1);
 Print(TestSymbol + ' ' + FormatFloat('#.####', R));
 IF (R > Value) AND (TestSymbol <> GetSymbol) THEN
 BEGIN
  CurrentSymbol := TestSymbol;
  Value := R;
```

```
 END;
END;
// end of "find the best correlated symbol" code
// ****************************************************************************
// ############################################################################
Stock1 := GetSymbol; // the symbol of the Price Series that is currently being
operated on
Stock2 := CurrentSymbol; // the symbol with the best correlation
// ############################################################################
// compute series
SetPrimarySeries( Stock1);
Close1 := #Close;
SetPrimarySeries( Stock2);
Close2 := #Close;
RestorePrimarySeries;
ActualRatioSeries := DivideSeries( Close1, Close2);
ActualRatioSMASeries := SMASeries( ActualRatioSeries, MAPeriod);
DeltaSeries := SubtractSeries( ActualRatioSeries, ActualRatioSMASeries);
DeltaSMASeries := SMASeries( DeltaSeries, MAPeriod);
DeltaDifferenceSeries := SubtractSeries( DeltaSeries, DeltaSMASeries);
DeltaNormSeries := DivideSeries( DeltaDifferenceSeries, StdDevSeries( DeltaSeries,
MAPeriod));
// correlation coefficient
Value := Correlation( Close1, Close2, 0, BarCount - 1);
// graphics
HideVolume;
EnableNotes(false);
RatioPane := CreatePane( 100, True, True);
PlotSeries( ActualRatioSeries, RatioPane, #Navy, #Thick);
PlotSeries( ActualRatioSMASeries, RatioPane, #Blue, #Thick);
DrawLabel('Ratio ' + Stock1 + '/' + Stock2 + ' and its '
    + IntToStr(MAPeriod) + ' Period Moving Average' , RatioPane);
StDevPane := CreatePane( 100, True, True);
PlotSeries( DeltaNormSeries, StDevPane, #Red, #ThickHist);
DrawHorzLine( Up_Threshold, StDevPane, #Black, #Thick);
DrawHorzLine( Down_Threshold, StDevPane, #Black, #Thick);
DrawHorzLine( Exit_Down_Threshold, StDevPane, #Blue, #Thick);
DrawHorzLine( Exit_Up_Threshold, StDevPane, #Blue, #Thick);
DrawLabel('no of standard deviations', StDevPane);
TextPane := CreatePane( 40, False, False);
DrawText( 'Correlation: ' + FormatFloat('0.####', Value), TextPane, 10, 10, #Black,
18 );
// procedures
```

```
PROCEDURE Close_Positions();
BEGIN
 if (ShortSymbol = Stock1) then LongSymbol := Stock2
  else LongSymbol := Stock1;
 SetPrimarySeries( ShortSymbol);
 CoverAtMarket( Bar + 1, LastPosition - 1, 'Cover ' + ShortSymbol);
 SetPrimarySeries( LongSymbol);
 SellAtMarket( Bar + 1, LastPosition, 'Sell ' + LongSymbol);
 RestorePrimarySeries;
END;
PROCEDURE Enter_Positions();
BEGIN
 if (ShortSymbol = Stock1) then LongSymbol := Stock2
  else LongSymbol := Stock1;
 SetPrimarySeries( ShortSymbol);
 if ShortSymbol = stock1 then
 ShortAtMarket( Bar + 1, 'ShortSell ' + ShortSymbol);
 SetPrimarySeries( LongSymbol);
 if longsymbol = stock1 then
 BuyAtMarket( Bar + 1, 'Buy ' + LongSymbol);
 RestorePrimarySeries;
END;
// main loop
FOR Bar := MAPeriod + 20 TO BarCount - 1 DO
BEGIN
  setprimaryseries(Stock2);
  atr2 := ATR(Bar - 1, 125);
  restoreprimaryseries();
  atr1 := ATR(Bar - 1, 125);
  if atr1 / priceclose(Bar - 1) > atr2 / GetSeriesValue(Bar - 1, Close2) * 1.0 then
  begin
  // applyautostops(Bar);
 IF LastPositionActive THEN
 BEGIN
   IF ((GetSeriesValue( Bar, DeltaNormSeries) < Exit_Up_Threshold) AND (ShortSymbol
= Stock1)) THEN
  BEGIN
   ShortSymbol := Stock1;
   Close_Positions();
  END; // < Exit_Up_Threshold
  IF ((GetSeriesValue( Bar, DeltaNormSeries) > Exit_Down_Threshold) AND
(ShortSymbol = Stock2)) THEN
  BEGIN
```

```
   ShortSymbol := Stock2;
   Close_Positions();
  END; // < Exit_Up_Threshold
END // if LastPositionActive
ELSE // no position active
BEGIN
 IF GetSeriesValue( Bar, DeltaNormSeries) > Up_Threshold THEN
 BEGIN
 if (priceclose(Bar)> priceclose(Bar - 1) * 1.02) then
  begin
   ShortSymbol := Stock1;
   Enter_Positions();
   end;
  END; // if > Up_Threshold
  IF GetSeriesValue( Bar, DeltaNormSeries) < Down_Threshold THEN
  BEGIN
   ShortSymbol := Stock2;
   if priceclose(bar) < priceclose(Bar - 1) * 0.98 then
   Enter_Positions();
  END; // if < Down_Threshold
 END; // else
END;
END;
```

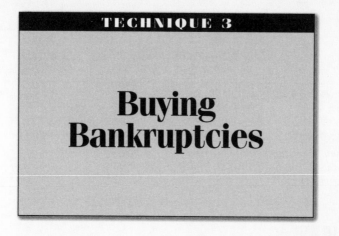

Buying Bankruptcies

Some of the best systems are discovered the hard way: by losing money. When United Airlines (UAL) went bankrupt on December 9, 2002, I was in the process of moving homes, and the next time I looked at the market, I noticed UAL had bounced from a low of 64 cents to over a dollar. I assumed that, of course, the market was happy to give me free money and I shorted at 1.09 only to watch it quickly go up to $2 a few days later.

When looking at more bankruptcies, I saw this was not an uncommon pattern. In many cases a company will go bankrupt, the stock will get halted, open much lower after the halt, and then promptly double. So many people had anticipated the bankruptcy, with the thought that the shares would then automatically be worth zero, that immediately after the halt is lifted, a short squeeze occurs.

Table 3.1 shows some recent large bankruptcies that were liquid enough after filing Technique 11 to trade around. The data are not significant, there being only six occurrences, and bankruptcies are seldom liquid enough to play. That said, I do think high profile bankruptcies will continue to fall under this pattern.

TABLE 3.1   Recent Bankruptcies

Stock	Date of Technique 11 Filing	Open After Halt Lifted ($)	High After Halt Lifted ($)	Return (%)
FAO Schwarz (FAOOQ)	1/13/02	0.25	0.63	152
UAL Corp. (UAL)	12/9/02	0.64	2.09	226
Kmart (KMRTQ)	1/22/02	0.70	1.63	133
Enron (ENRNQ)	12/3/01	0.26	1.26	385
WorldCom (WCOEQ)	7/21/02	0.08	0.17	113
US Airways	8/14/02	0.25	0.75	200

EXAMPLES

UAL

UAL filed for Chapter 11 on December 9, 2002. The stock opened that day at 0.64. By December 13, the stock was at 2.09. (See Figure 3.1.)

Kmart

Kmart had been in a losing battle for several years to avoid bankruptcy, and finally on January 22, 2002, it happened. After the halt, the stock reopened at 70 cents and six trading days later on January 30 it reached a high of 1.63. (See Figure 3.2, page 52.)

WCOM

WCOM disintegrated into thin air in the first half of 2002. In February of 2002 I had been playing a mean reversion system on stocks and had bought WCOM in the 6s and sold a week later in the 9s. I was feeling pretty good about myself at the time, but there was one moment when I was reading an article in *Fortune* magazine about how the credit derivatives of WCOM were basically crashing even as the stock was going up. I was thinking to myself, how could that be? I had perused some of their filings and had determined that although they had a plate full of debt, hardly any of it was due for at least a year. Corruption explained things pretty quickly, and a short while later the stock was trading near zero. (See Figure 3.3, page 53.)

WCOM filed for bankruptcy on July 21, 2002, and the next day the stock opened at 10 cents. A day later it hit a high of 21 cents, over 100 percent higher.

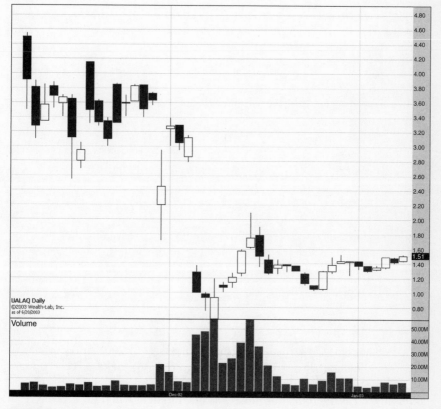

FIGURE 3.1 UAL.

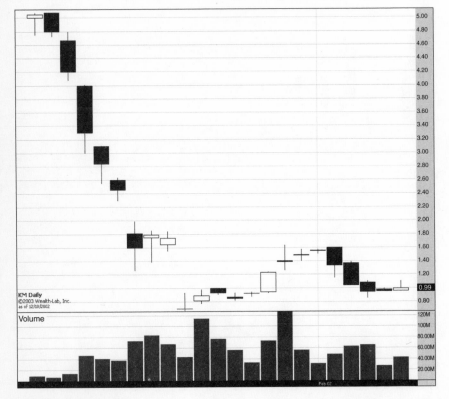

FIGURE 3.2   Kmart.

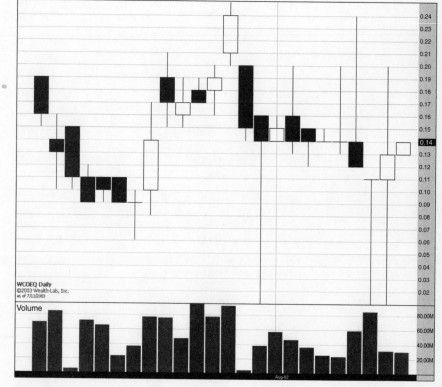

FIGURE 3.3 WCOM.

Now, one can argue, 10 cents? How can I make any money on that? And if you argue that in general, then you are probably right. However, in this case, the volume was over 70M shares on both the day the halt was lifted and the day after. The average investor using a direct access broker (and paying $5 commissions one way) could have easily picked up 100,000 shares or more in either direction. Not bad for one day's work.

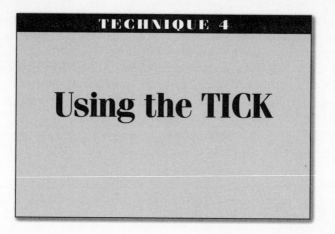

TECHNIQUE 4

Using the TICK

While there are many sentiment indicators out there—put/call ratio, the VIX, the advance/decline line, and so on—the New York Stock Exchange (NYSE) TICK indicator is perhaps the rawest expression of investor sentiment at any given second during the day. The TICK can be used to generate trades designed to profit from intraday shifts in sentiment. In this technique I describe two systems for working such trades.

The NYSE TICK indicator represents the number of stocks that ticked upward (within the past second) minus the number of stocks that ticked downward. For instance, if the TICK is at +300, then 300 more stocks upticked than downticked within the past second. At that moment, the market is most likely moving upward, since 300 more stocks are moving up than down. If the TICK is at –300, then at that moment 300 more stocks had just downticked than upticked. If the TICK is at –300, the market is probably moving down at that moment.

During a typical day, the TICK ranges from +400 to –400. Extreme readings can get as high as +1,000 and –1,000. In the week after September 11, 2001, there were many cases of extreme –1,000 readings. Similarly, in the comeback period after that week, +1,000 was not uncommon. Readings of greater than +1,000 are considered to represent overbought conditions because supposedly too many companies are upticking. Readings of –1,000 represent oversold conditions because supposedly too many companies are downticking. It is at those moments of panic that we look for opportunity.

Likewise, if the TICK is steadily negative for an entire half hour without any real positive movement, this position also might indicate an oversold condition—too many people have sold in panic. Or if the TICK is steadily positive for an entire half hour without any real negative movement, that might indicate an overbought condition. These conditions are what I utilize in the system described immediately following.

For all of the tests and charts in my intraday TICK system, I am using one-half hour data starting at 9:30 AM and continuing throughout the day until 4 PM. The first half hour of the day goes from 9:30 AM to 10 AM, the second goes from 10 AM to 10:30 AM, and so on. You can use various charting software packages to keep track of the half-hour bars on the TICK and other equities.

THE INTRADAY TICK SYSTEM

- Buy when in any half-hour bar, the high of the TICK is –50, then wait until the next half-hour bar begins and buy QQQ when it goes lower than the low of the previous half-hour bar.
- *Sell* immediately when the trade is 2 percent profitable. Or when the TICK has hit a high of at least 400, sell at the end of the half-hour bar. Or if 10 hours have passed (during which the market is open—ignore overnight hours) without either of the previous two conditions having occurred, then sell immediately.

Examples

On August 8, 2002, the market was not in good shape. It had made a multiyear low on July 24, 2002, and then bounced—but the worst was yet to come. Every other week new economic reports were showing global economic collapse, deflation, inflation, and so on. I would wake up at 3 in the morning to check the Nikkei only to see it making another 17-year low. (I can't even remember back 17 years let alone think about the horror of a market that is breaking even with where it was 17 years ago.) I would then check Stephen Roach's latest column on the Morgan Stanley Web site only to see him proclaim yet again that the economic condition of the United States was similar to where it was in 1931 (despite the fact that we had 25 percent unemployment then.)

Meanwhile, Pakistan and India were dancing around the issue of nuclear war, people were obsessed with when the next terrorist attack would occur on U.S. soil, and George Soros was saying the U.S. dollar was going to go into a death spiral. So what did people do for fun during these heady times? They sold stocks—by the truckload.

Trading QQQ (August 2, 2002)   Figure 4.1 shows the behavior of QQQ over the course of August 2, 2002. The line in the top pane represents

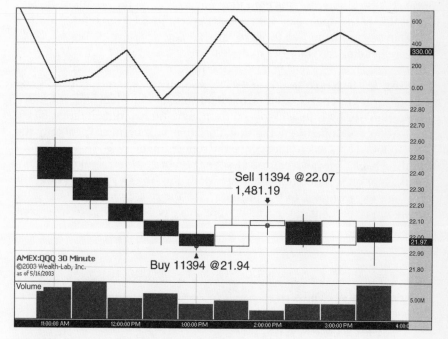

FIGURE 4.1 Trading QQQ, August 2002.

the high point for each half hour in the NYSE TICK. The bars in the bottom pane are the volume during the half-hour bars on QQQ. (The bars go from 10:30 AM to 4 PM.) The middle pane represents the high and low price on QQQ during each half hour. You will notice that QQQ goes from about 22.60 to 21.90, while the high for each half hour on the TICK goes back and forth between +600 and −100.

For the half hour between 12:00 and 12:30, all the remaining buyers apparently went to lunch and the TICK never caught its breath above −100 for that period. At 12:30 it continued to dip and the system bought at 21.94. Between 1:00 and 1:30 the TICK reached a high of +400 without the QQQs hitting the profit target. This condition means that on the next bar we take our profits at the open, 22.07, for a 0.59 percent profit in an hour.

Things went from bad to worse after August, and by October 7, 2002, we were heading into another multiyear low.

Trading QQQ (October 7, 2002)   As you can see in Figure 4.2 (see page 60), on October 7, 2002, from 3:00 to 3:30 the TICK did not move higher than −100. From 3:30 to 4:00 we bought the continued dip at 20.00. The market continued to spike down another half percent (probably the panic induced by weak holders once the round number was broken) before bouncing back. The next day, on October 8, shortly after the open, and before the market went on to make a new daily low, the QQQ hit our target at 20.40 and we were out of the position. See the results in Table 4.1. As it turned out, 80 percent of the trades were successful, with an average profit of 0.88 percent per trade.

TABLE 4.1 Intraday TICK System: Trading QQQ, March 24, 1999 to June 30, 2003	
	All Trades
Total Number of Trades	46
Average Profit/Loss %	0.88%
Average Bars Held	5.61
Winning Trades	37 (80.43%)
Average Profit %	1.51%
Average Bars Held	4.43
Maximum Consecutive Winning Trades	13
Losing Trades	9 (19.57%)
Average Loss %	−1.73%
Average Bars Held	10.44
Maximum Consecutive Losing Trades	3

Trading NVDA (October 7, 2002)   This system can also be used with volatile stocks, such as NVDA. The chart in Figure 4.3 (see page 61) is the same day as the previous trade, but instead of analyzing QQQ, it charts Nvidia (NVDA:Nasdaq). As you can see, the system catches NVDA in the bar between 3:30 and 4:00 PM at $7.70. The next day it gaps up in the morning at 7.96. We are out by 8:30 AM. See the results in Table 4.2.

TABLE 4.2   Intraday TICK System: Trading NVDA, January 1, 1999 to June 30, 1999

	All Trades
Total Number of Trades	34
Average Profit/Loss %	1.28%
Average Bars Held	3.74
Winning Trades	29 (85.29%)
Average Profit %	1.86%
Average Bars Held	2.93
Maximum Consecutive Winning Trades	16
Losing Trades	5 (14.71%)
Average Loss %	−2.12%
Average Bars Held	8.4
Maximum Consecutive Losing Trades	2

THE INTRADAY TICK SYSTEM VARIATION: THE LOW-GRADE PANIC ATTACK

Sometimes the market does not spike down but, instead, does a steady sell-off that lasts for hours. Being long at those points and staring at the quote screen is beyond painful. Better to get a basketball and shoot hoops for a few hours. Then come back to your desk. If the market has been steadily selling off the entire time, then there might be an opportunity to play the following system.

- Buy when five half-hour bars in a row on the TICK chart have a low TICK reading below –400, then wait until the next half hour bar and buy when the QQQ hits a five-bar low.
- Sell when the position is 1 percent profitable, then sell immediately, or when the TICK goes greater than 400, then sell at the end of that

FIGURE 4.2   Trading QQQ, October 2002.

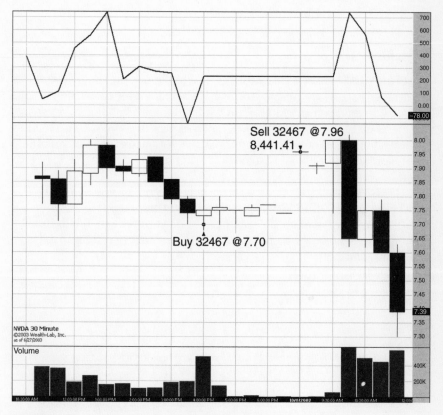

FIGURE 4.3 Trading NVDA, October 2002.

half-hour bar or, if four days have passed without either of the other conditions occurring, then sell at the end of the day.

The basic idea is that we are looking for times when there has been relentless selling for two hours. Every time the market tries to rally, it gets hit down again, and again, and again. Finally, the only longs left on the day are somewhat stronger than the weak longs who sold earlier. This circumstance does not mean the market is going up, but it does increase our chances of getting a favorable bounce.

Example

Trading QQQ (March 25, 2002) The top line in the first panel of Figure 4.4 (see page 64) represents the high TICK reading for each half hour; the bottom line represents the low TICK reading for each half hour. As you can see, at 12 noon the market had just had five bars in a row of extreme low TICK readings. This condition means that at least once every half hour there was heavy selling. Enough to make a grown man cry if you were long tech stocks.

The system picks up a potential trade between after the end of the five bars between 10 AM and 12:30 PM. It sets the buy price at $35.77, the five-bar low (i.e., the low between 10:00 and 12:30). That order gets filled. Holding for the 1 percent profit takes us to $36.13 less than two hours later (between 2:00 and 2:30).

Altogether, this system succeeds close to 80 percent of the time with an average expected value of 0.50 percent per trade, as you can see from Table 4.3.

TABLE 4.3 Intraday TICK System 2: Trading QQQ
(March 1999 to June 2003)

	All Trades
Total Number of Trades	174
Average Profit/Loss %	0.50%
Average Bars Held	4.82
Winning Trades	136 (78.16%)
Average Bars Held	3.59
Maximum Consecutive Winning Trades	21
Losing Trades	38 (21.84%)
Average Bars Held	9.21
Maximum Consecutive Losing Trades	5

TABLE 4.4 Intraday TICK System 2: Trading QQQ with TICK Bar < –600 (March 1999 to June 2003)

	All Trades
Total Number of Trades	33
Average Profit/Loss %	0.85%
Average Bars Held	4.12
Winning Trades	31 (93.94%)
Average Profit %	0.97%
Average Bars Held	3.26
Maximum Consecutive Winning Trades	15
Losing Trades	2 (6.06%)
Average Loss %	–1.12
Average Bars Held	17.5
Maximum Consecutive Losing Trades	1

To increase both the odds of success and the expected value per trade, you can do any of three things:

1. Lower the TICK bar. Instead of looking for multiple –400 readings, look for multiple –600 readings.
2. Wait for more confirming bars. Instead of buying after five bars of low readings, wait for six or more bars. Or wait until these readings occur after an already negative day.
3. Buy on the sixth bar at a 10-bar low instead of a 5-bar low.

For example, executing the system just described—except looking for multiple TICK readings less than –600 instead of –400—has the result on QQQ shown in Table 4.4. The odds increase to 94 percent, and the expected value per trade goes to 0.85 percent. The downside is that you get far fewer trades.

CONCLUSION

One thing to note is that applying the rules described in this technique in reverse does not work for shorting. Why? I don't know. Maybe it is just not healthy to fade too much happiness. It could also be that at moments when the TICK is greater than, say, 1,000 (representing an extreme in buying), too many people are already shorting, and when the next highs are reached in

FIGURE 4.4   Trading QQQ, March 2002.

the market the shortsellers begin to get squeezed, propelling the market further. Whatever the case, the TICK is best used to measure fear rather than greed. These extreme moments of fear do not just occur in bear markets. In 1994, 1997, 1998, and 1999, the market hit extreme low points. Volatility and panic are facts of life, not just outliers inside of bear markets.

The TICK is the rawest measure of panic we can possibly have in the market. Every second it boils down the fear in the marketplace into a single number. Buying those extreme moments can pay off.

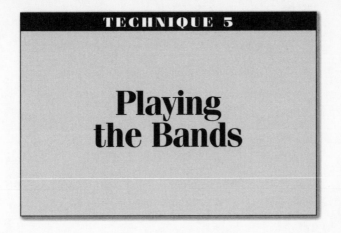

TECHNIQUE 5

Playing the Bands

Bollinger bands, named after John Bollinger who was the first to widely use and write about them, are trading bands around the moving average of a stock that are commonly used to determine oversold or overbought conditions. They are calculated by taking the moving average of a stock (10 for short-term periods, 20 for intermediate-term, 100 or 200 for longer-term) and then surrounding that moving average with an upper band and lower band signifying x number of standard deviations around the moving average.

As an example, Figure 5.1 shows the Bollinger bands for CHKP using the 20-day moving average and 2 standard deviations.

The basic idea for using Bollinger bands is that when a stock hits the upper band, it is usually overbought so you should short, and when a stock hits the lower band, it is usually oversold, so you should buy. The rationale is that price tends to revert to its moving average.

BOLLINGER BAND SYSTEM #1

- Buy when a stock hits the lower band using a 20-day moving average and 2 standard deviations.
- Sell when a stock returns to its moving average.

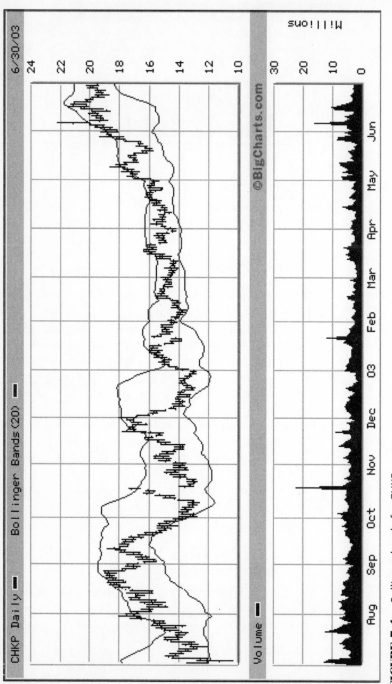

FIGURE 5.1 Bollinger bands for CHKP.

Example: CHKP, 7/11/2001

On July 7, 2001, CHKP (shown in Figure 5.2) gapped down and proceeded to hit its lower Bollinger Band at 40.45. The system held the position until July 27 at 42.69 for a 5.51 percent profit. (See Table 5.1 for results.)

TABLE 5.1 Basic Bollinger Band System: Nasdaq 100 Stocks, January 1, 1998 to June 1, 2003

	All Trades
All Trades	3,352
Average Profit/Loss %	1.96%
Average Bars Held	9.38
Winning Trades	2428 (72.43%)
Average Profit %	7.32%
Average Bars Held	5.21
Maximum Consecutive Winning Trades	63
Losing Trades	924 (27.57%)
Average Loss %	−12.12%
Average Bars Held	20.35
Maximum Consecutive Losing Trades	15

The basic idea holds up and delivers a fairly consistent return with a high probability. There are several twists that I do on the basic system to improve both the odds of success and the percent return per trade. For one thing, I do not like to wait for the stock to return to its moving average. Even if a company is in big trouble, even going bankrupt (and see Technique 3 on bankruptcies for an example of what I am about to say), stocks do not move in a straight line. The faster the spike down, the more likely the stock is to do a quick bounce up. However, if the company is truly in trouble, over time the stock will do its little spike up and then drift down, bringing the moving average, and the potential for profit, down with it.

SHORT-TERM BOLLINGER BAND SYSTEM WITH PROFIT TARGET

Not only am I interested in if the stock simply touches the Bollinger band, but if it decisively breaks through it, which introduces the concept of "percent b." Percent b (%b) is the percent level the stock price is at relative to its bands. If the stock is dead center between the bands, then the %b = 50.

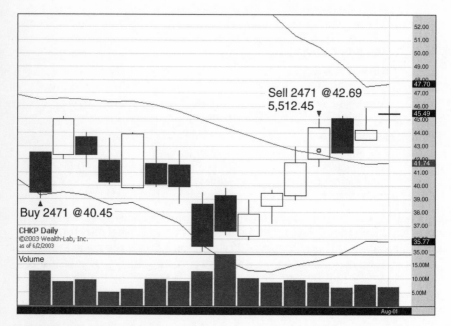

FIGURE 5.2   CHKP on July 11, 2001.

If the stock is touching the upper band, then the %b is 100, and if it is below the lower band, then the %b is negative. The following formula is used to calculate %b:

$$100 \left(\frac{\text{Stock Price} - \text{Lower Band}}{\text{Upper Band} - \text{Lower Band}} \right)$$

Which all leads to the following:

- Buy when %b is less than –20 using Bollinger Bands on the 10-day moving average with 1.5 standard deviations and hold at least until the close of that day even if profit target is hit.
- Sell when either a 15 percent profit target is hit or four days go by, whichever comes first.

With this system, we are using the 10-day moving average to get quicker and sharper spikes. We use a –20 %b to make sure it is a decisive break of the bands. And if we don't get our target within four days, then we are run like hell out of the trade.

Example: SEBL, 8/31/98

August 31, 1998. The markets had been in turmoil all summer, culminating in the Long Term Capital Crisis. Panic had set in and everyone was worried the party was over. After nine down days in a row, during four of which the lower Bollinger Band was broken through, the stock price finally hit our buy target at 4.81 on August 31. The next day it bounced, hitting a 15 percent target at 5.54 (see Figure 5.3).

Example: BRCD, 4/14/2000

April 14, 2000, was not a pleasant day to be long tech stocks. In fact, it seemed like the world might quite possibly end. At the time I was working at 44 Wall Street, and when I left the building that evening pedestrians were jokingly being warned to stay away from the sidewalks just in case people were jumping out of buildings. Nevertheless, despite the pain, it was certainly an important day to be buying short-term moves in stocks. As shown in Figure 5.4, on that day, BRCD triggered a buy signal at 46.42. It started to make a comeback on Monday the 17th and finally hit the 15 percent profit target on the 18th at 53.38. (See results in Table 5.2, page 74.)

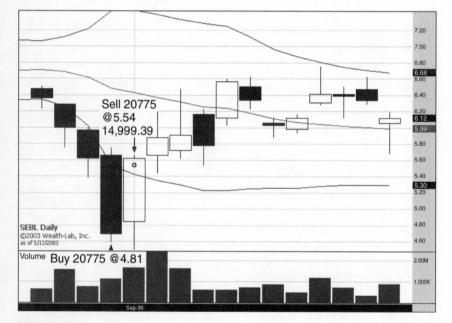

FIGURE 5.3   SEBL on August 31, 1998.

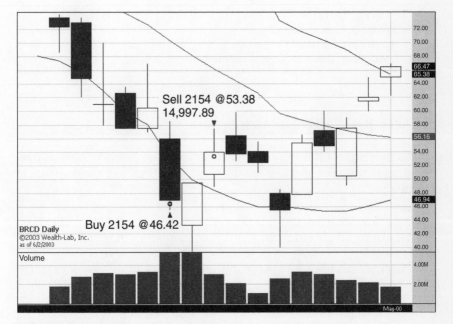

FIGURE 5.4 BRCD on April 14, 2000.

TABLE 5.2   Short-Term Bollinger Band System: Nasdaq 100
Stocks, January 1, 1998 to June 1, 2003

	All Trades
All Trades	265
Average Profit/Loss %	8.66%
Average Bars Held	2.46
Winning Trades	202 (76.23%)
Average Profit %	14.75%
Average Bars Held	1.98
Maximum Consecutive Winning Trades	21
Losing Trades	63 (23.77%)
Average Loss %	−10.87%
Average Bars Held	4
Maximum Consecutive Losing Trades	3

WHAT ABOUT SHORTING?

Just as the markets rarely go down in a straight line, neither do they go up
in a straight line. For shorting, try the short-term Bollinger Band system in
reverse:

- Short a stock when its %b is greater than 120 using Bollinger Bands on
  the 10-day moving average with 1.5 standard deviations.
- Hold at least until the close of that day even if profit target is hit.
- Cover when either a 15 percent profit target is hit or four days go by,
  whichever comes first.

Example: NVDA, 8/19/99

As can be imagined, there were a lot of examples to short in 1999 when the
Internet bubble was in full force. Look at Figure 5.5. NVDA, a darling not
only during the bubble but also in the down years of 2000 and 2001, shot up
on August 19, 1999, and crossed its upper band by over 20 percent, upon
which event a short signal results at 6.80 before going a further 5 percent at
7.09. Four days later the trade is closed out at 6.25 for an 8 percent profit.

The results as shown in Table 5.3 are not that great really: 1.50% per
trade, which is fine, but only a small number of trades compared to other
systems we have looked at with similar profit per trade results. Also, prob-

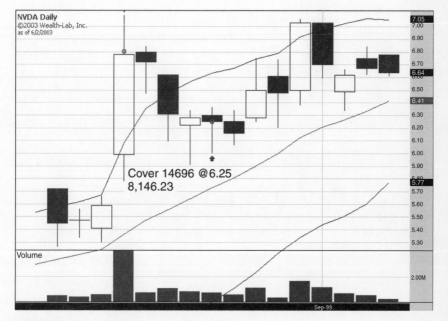

FIGURE 5.5 NVDA on August 19, 1999.

TABLE 5.3   Bollinger Band Shorting System: Trading NVDA, August 19, 1999

	All Trades
All Trades	219
Average Profit/Loss %	1.50%
Average Bars Held	3.59
Winning Trades	139 (63.47%)
Average Profit %	9.79%
Average Bars Held	3.35
Maximum Consecutive Winning Tables	11
Losing Trades	80 (36.53%)
Average Loss %	−12.91%
Average Bars Held	4.01
Maximum Consecutive Losing Trades	6

ability is not as high as in some of the other Bollinger Band systems described in this technique.

While in general I could care less whether I am going long or shorting, the reality is that shorting is not the opposite of going long. It is more like a distant second cousin of going long; a weaker version that seldom works, even after extreme moves.

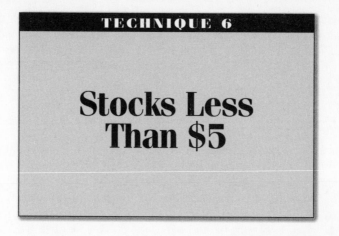

TECHNIQUE 6

Stocks Less Than $5

I nvestors as a rule shun low-priced stocks (stocks trading for less than $5). Using a Google search for "stocks less than 5" and "low-priced stocks," I came across dozens of articles, newsletters, advisory services, and so on that stated that buying low-priced stocks was the quickest way to ruin. Some of the common reasons include:

- Stocks never come back once they go below $5.
- Stocks are more easily manipulated below $5.
- Stocks go below $5 "for a reason."

However, this is all good news for the hedge fund trader. The fear that is spread throughout the marketplace about low-priced stocks translates into a higher-risk premium and, as a category, these low-priced stocks tends to do well and are important trading vehicles.

EXAMPLES

OVER, 12/21/01

OVER was still called GoTo.com in late 2001, and the dot-com backlash was still happening big-time across the market. GoTo.com could not figure out its business model (Was it a search engine? Was it a collection of high-traffic sites selling advertising?), and the market was not tolerating its indecision. The stock slid all through December ("tax selling," the message board posters on Yahoo! tried to claim in defense), and it seemed like there was no hope for the stock—until it hit 5 bucks a share to make a 52-week low on December 21, 2001 (Figure 6.1). Buying at $5 and holding for one month would have allowed you to sell on January 24, 2002, at 12.19 for a 143 percent profit.

INFT, 9/30/02

INFT, Inforte, describes itself as "a customer and demand management consultancy," which seems to be an obscure way of saying they are an information technology (IT) services company. Demand for IT services had fallen for two straight years, and the environment was not getting any better. Many of the companies that had gone public around the same time as INFT had gone bankrupt or had been bought for pennies. INFT crossed below $5 on 9/30 and then hit a 52-week low on October 3, 2002, when it went as low as $4.75. Nevertheless, the company had $50M cash in the bank, no debt, and was trading at a $50M market cap at that price. And was profitable! Buying at $5 a share, holding for one month and selling on October 29, 2002, would have allowed you to book a 56 percent profit (see Figure 6.2).

However, not everything is so rosy in low-priced land as the following example shows.

WCOM, 4/10/02

WCOM basically disintegrated overnight as a company. I remember reading an interview in the spring of 2002 with a fairly prominent value investor who was saying "people are just now starting to realize WCOM is a value stock. We can easily see it double or triple from here." Within months people realized that WCOM had committed billions of dollars worth of fraud. It is hard to make money on the long side in the face of massive fraud. (Although Technique 3 on bankruptcies describes how you could have made money shortly after WCOM filed for Chapter 11.)

On April 10, 2002, WCOM hit below $5 for the first time that year (Figure 6.3, page 83). Within a week it looked like there might be a chance at recovery as the shares went as high as $7. Nevertheless, holding for one month would have cost 60 percent of your investment as you would have sold at 2.01 on May 9, 2002.

FIGURE 6.1   OVER on December 21, 2001.

FIGURE 6.2   INFT on September 30, 2002.

FIGURE 6.3　WCOM on April 10, 2002.

BUY LESS THAN $5

The WCOM example clearly shows the risk of playing low-priced stocks. And, INFT aside, the difficulty in differentiating between the potential WCOMs and the potential OVERs makes it hard to justify buying any stock from a fundamental or technical perspective. That said, the following system produces some interesting results:

- Buy when the 52-week low of the stock is greater than 5 or buy the moment the stock crosses below $5.
- Sell one month later.

For results, see Table 6.1, which shows an average return of 11.2 percent per trade versus an average monthly return of approximately 0 percent across the universe of stocks since 1998.

TABLE 6.1 Data on 7000 Stocks Including All NYSE, Nasdaq, AMEX Stocks Including Deletions, January 1, 1998 to January 1, 2003	
	All Trades
All Trades	1,886
Average Profit/Loss %	11.2%
Winning Trades	1110 (58.85%
Average Profit %	33.25%
Maximum Consecutive Winning Trades	23
Losing Trades	776 (41.15%)
Average Loss %	−20.21%
Maximum Consecutive Losing Trades	17

CONCLUSION

The key is to use very small amounts of equity per trade. Since so many trades are generated, there is no shortage of ideas for putting money to work.

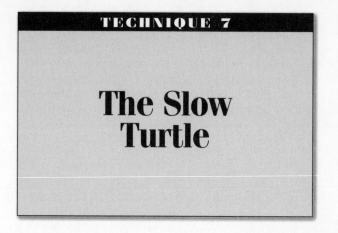

TECHNIQUE 7

The Slow Turtle

Probably no trading system in existence has produced as much cult-like fervor as the Turtle trading system originally developed by Richard Dennis and William Eckhardt and now being used by possibly hundreds of hedge funds to manage currencies, stocks, and commodities. The original story goes that Eckhardt was convinced that trading couldn't be taught and Dennis was convinced it could be. They made a bet and then used very minimal criteria to select a group of students to teach. These students became the original "turtles" (named after the Turtle system that they were taught) and most of them went on to manage fairly impressive funds. All of them were sworn to secrecy about the details of the original system. However, I doubt at this point any of them use that original system and if they do, it is certainly not the version we want to be using, the Turtles trade trends.

Basically, if a commodity or stock is breaking to new highs, the idea is that that momentum should continue and you should just ride the asset until it is no longer making new highs. By trading a basket of uncorrelated markets, you can take advantage of the fact that at any given point, somewhere in the financial universe, something is in a bull market.

Trend-following can offer huge returns. If you catch close to the beginning of a huge bull move in a market, the returns on that trade can be multiples of 100 percent. Similarly, the drawdowns can be enormous. Dennis himself has gone in and out of the hedge fund business several times, most recently closing shop in 2000, primarily because his drawdowns have been immense and clients have withdrawn money. The key to success in a trend-following system is not in picking the right entries and exits, but merely staying in the game to be able to withstand the drawdowns. That said, if one chooses a basket of assets carefully so that they are as uncorrelated as possible, it may be possible to smooth out drawdowns. We will see a simple example of that possibility in a bit.

MY VERSION OF THE TURTLE SYSTEM

As for the system itself, there are many variations of the basic Turtle system and its trend-following cousins. The version presented here is based on one told to me by a manager of a multibillion-dollar trend-following fund. Although most of the systems presented in this book are short-term countertrend systems, I do think a properly diversified trading strategy should include some trend-following component. This is the system I currently use:

- Buy if an asset's 22-week closing simple moving average crosses over its 55-week closing moving average; buy at the market open the next Monday.
- Sell if an asset's 22-week closing simple moving average crosses under its 55-week closing moving average; sell at the market open the next Monday.

Note the simplicity of the method. The more complicated a system is, the more likely it is to suffer from severe curve fitting. Basically, I am not as interested in using complicated methods from quantum mechanics to identify trends. If an asset is moving up so that its slow- and fast-moving averages are moving up, then I am happy to say it is trending.

Why no shorting? As we have seen in Technique 5, shorting is not necessarily the opposite of going long. Along with the fact that the markets have a natural bias to move upward over the past one hundred years, your upside is also capped at a 100 percent. When following a long-term trend-following system, it is possible to have trades that make well over 100 percent. Also, if you choose your basket of assets correctly, you can be going long some assets, while other assets are on their downtrends.

EXAMPLES

S&P 500, June 1958 to June 1961

The lowest line in Figure 7.1 represents the 55-week moving average. The line directly above it represents the 22-week exponential moving average. On June 23, 1958, the lines crossed, and we bought at the open of the next

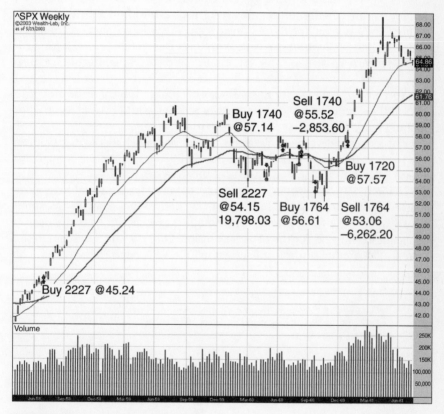

FIGURE 7.1 S&P 500, 1958–1961.

week holding until the bottom line crossed under on May 2, 1960, when we closed out the trade for a 19.6 percent profit. The market seesawed for a year or so afterwards before we bought again on January 3, 1961, at the start of the next bull market that lasted throughout the 1960s.

S&P 500, July 1987 to May, 2003

Of course, no trend-following system would be worth its weight in salt if it did not capture the trend that occurred throughout the 1990s as shown in Figure 7.2. As seen in the figure, the system was long the market from February 19, 1991, right after the Gulf War, until December 11, 2000, for a 271 percent return. (Also see Table 7.1, Table 7.2 (page 88), and Table 7.3 (page 89).)

You can, of course, run this system on stocks. Table 7.3 shows the results of the system on Nasdaq 100 stocks, starting with $1M and using 2 percent of equity per trade.

The system was almost always in the market and had, of course, its equity peak at the peak of the bull market in 2000 (see Figure 7.3, page 90). Figure 7.4 shows the annual returns of the system.

Using the Turtle system on stocks, you would have been able to maximize the advantages of the bull market while keeping drawdowns somewhat low in the bear market even though they existed. Notably, despite being a horrible year for the broader market, 2001 was up 8 percent in this system. The annual returns are shown in Table 7.4, page 93.

TABLE 7.1	Results for the Turtle System on the S&P 500, 1950 to 2003
	All Trades
All Trades	16
Average Profit/Loss	$29,217.51
Average Profit/Loss %	29.26%
Average Bars Held	123.63
Winning Trades	12 (75.00%)
Average Profit %	41.14%
Average Bars Held	158.5
Maximum Consecutive Winning Trades	10
Losing Trades	4 (25.00%)
Average Loss %	–6.39%
Average Bars Held	19
Maximum Consecutive Losing Trades	2

FIGURE 7.2 S&P 500, 1987–2003.

TABLE 7.2   Trades for Slow Turtle on S&P

Position	Symbol	Shares	Entry Date	Entry Price	Exit Date	Exit Price	% Change
Long	^SPX	3,929	8/4/1952	25.43	6/15/1953	23.62	−7.12
Long	^SPX	3,868	1/25/1954	25.93	2/18/1957	43.46	67.61
Long	^SPX	2,118	5/27/1957	46.78	9/30/1957	42.42	−9.32
Long	^SPX	2,227	6/30/1958	45.24	5/2/1960	54.13	19.65
Long	^SPX	1,740	6/20/1960	57.16	8/8/1960	55.52	−2.87
Long	^SPX	1,764	8/15/1960	56.61	9/26/1960	53.06	−6.27
Long	^SPX	1,720	1/3/1961	57.57	6/4/1962	59.12	2.69
Long	^SPX	1,508	2/4/1963	66.31	6/20/1966	86.51	30.46
Long	^SPX	1,124	3/13/1967	88.89	7/22/1969	94.95	6.82
Long	^SPX	1,085	1/4/1971	92.15	6/11/1973	107.03	16.15
Long	^SPX	1,104	5/12/1975	90.53	5/31/1977	96.27	6.34
Long	^SPX	1,024	7/17/1978	97.58	9/28/1981	112.77	15.57
Long	^SPX	748	10/18/1982	133.59	6/18/1984	149.03	11.56
Long	^SPX	596	8/27/1984	167.51	12/7/1987	223.98	33.71
Long	^SPX	359	10/10/1988	278.06	9/24/1990	311.3	11.95
Long	^SPX	270	2/19/1991	369.06	12/11/2000	1,369.89	271.18

Looking at Figure 7.5 (see page 92), an analysis of the maximum adverse excursion (the amount a trade went negative before closing out), the light gray trades represent the trades that eventually were closed out as profitable trades but underwent a drawdown in the process. One trade was as much as 40 percent down before returning to profitability, and 17 trades were between 20 percent and 40 percent down before returning to profitability. We can see in the results that the maximum drawdown from peak to low was slightly over 58 percent. Nevertheless, this system greatly outperformed the market from 1998 to 2003 and was able to benefit massively during extreme bull market moves. Again, having a trend-following system in your arsenal is an important weapon in addition to the various countertrend systems we have demonstrated in this book.

TABLE 7.3 Simulation of Slow Turtle on NAS 100 Stocks (1997–2003)

	All Trades
Starting Capital	$1,000,000.00
Ending Capital	$5,423,025.50
Net Profit	$4,423,025.50
Net Profit %	442.30%
Exposure %	91.32%
Risk-Adjusted Return	484.34%
All Trades	213
Average Profit/Loss	$20,765.38
Average Profit/Loss %	85.84%
Average Bars Held	59.24
Winning Trades	107 (50.23%)
Gross Profit	$6,383,812.50
Average Profit	$59,661.80
Average Profit %	193.19%
Average Bars Held	80.11
Maximum Consecutive Winning Trades	14
Losing Trades	106 (49.77%)
Gross Loss	($1,960,787.38)
Average Loss	($18,497.99)
Average Loss %	−22.52%
Average Bars Held	38.18
Maximum Consecutive Losing Trades	13
Maximum Drawdown	−58.44%
Maximum Drawdown $	($6,169,147.50)
Maximum Drawdown Date	9/17/2001
Recovery Factor	0.72
Profit Factor	3.26

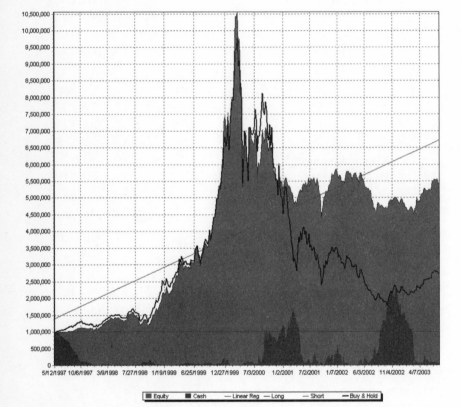

FIGURE 7.3   Portfolio equity curve.

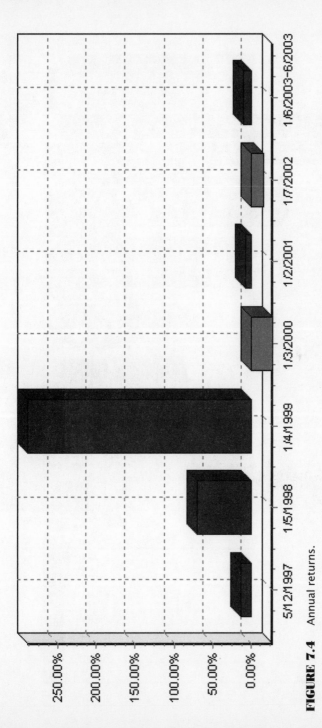

FIGURE 7.4 Annual returns.

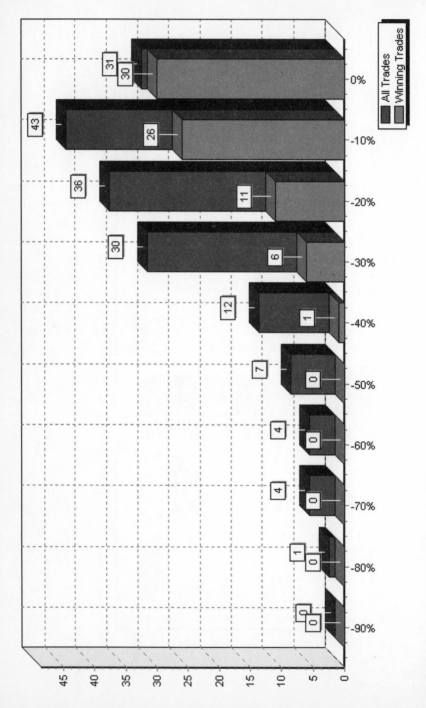

FIGURE 7.5 Maximum adverse excursion.

| **TABLE 7.4** | Annual Returns for Slow Turtle on NASDAQ 100 Stocks | | |

| | | % Maximum | | |
	$ Return	% Return	DD	Exposure
1997	128,279.75	12.83	−7.18	58.92
1998	790,990.50	70.11	−27.27	97.45
1999	5,539,361.00	288.62	−15.72	98.68
2000	−2,028,572.00	−27.2	−49.43	94.97
2001	433,967.50	7.99	−21.69	90.35
2002	−953,636.00	−16.26	−21.92	86.32
2003*	512,632.00	10.44	−8.98	90.43

*Only until June 2003.

A Basket of Uncorrelated Stocks

Let us do a similar analysis on a basket of stocks that are largely uncorrelated: two technology stocks (MSFT and INTC), two utilities (ED and SO), two commodity stocks (NEM [gold] and PAAS [silver]), and two industrials (AA and MMM). Using 30 percent of equity per trade, we get annual returns as shown in Figure 7.6 and Table 7.5. Using uncorrelated assets, even on a basket with only eight assets, is enough to significantly smooth out returns, particularly in bearish periods in the markets.

| **TABLE 7.5** | Annual Returns Using Slow Turtle on Basket of Uncorrelated Stocks | | | |

| | | | % Maximum | |
Period Starting	$ Return	% Return	DD	Exposure
4/22/1996	282,569.38	28.26	−2.19	29.3
1/6/1997	201,998.25	15.75	−11.91	76.96
1/5/1998	468,115.38	31.53	−6.8	55.74
1/4/1999	112,452.25	5.76	−13.91	66.15
1/3/2000	36,308.50	1.76	−33.53	67.09
1/2/2001	329,090.25	15.66	−6.33	69.04
1/7/2002	−12,389.75	−0.51	−18.54	68.78
1/6/2003*	256,371.75	10.6	−4.41	82.01

*Through June 2003.

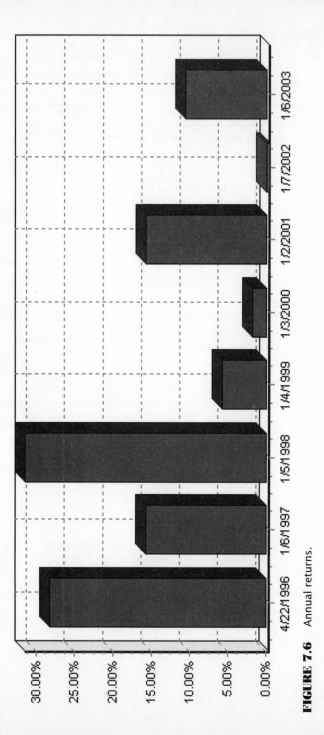

FIGURE 7.6   Annual returns.

OTHER VARIATIONS

There are many different variations on the Turtle system. A few of them are:

- Using a different type of moving average. The simple moving average (SMA) tends to identify trends a bit slowly. The exponential moving average or weighted moving average weights current data higher than older data and will signal a trend sooner than the SMA. That said, they are also prone to more whipsawing. If you are of the rocket scientist sort, you can play with the mesa adaptive moving average developed by John Ehlers and discussed in his book *Rocket Science for Traders* (Wiley, 2001).
- Pyramiding bets. The original Turtle system places some emphasis on money management, in particular, being able to pyramid the bet as the trend keeps moving in the original direction. Since a trend-following system is but one component of my trading, I do not feel pyramiding is necessary. Also, the volatility in today's markets is such that the drawdown potential is beyond immense if one is pyramiding bets. It is a guarantee that your largest loss will also be your last.
- Buying on a breakout of a recent high. Rather than using a moving average crossover, you can also buy the market on a breakout of a recent high. For instance, buy a breakout of a 20-bar high plus some multiple of the ATR (average true range).

Just as an aside, it is interesting to see what types of assets tend to trend. For instance, Figure 7.7 shows the federal funds rate from June 1987 to April 2003.

CONCLUSION

I have seen variations of the turtle system printed on various Web sites claiming to have the original Turtle system. It is a worthwhile exercise to test this system and its variants on stocks and confirm for yourself that they do not work. Note, however, that the Turtle system defined in this technique captured the tops and bottoms very nicely.

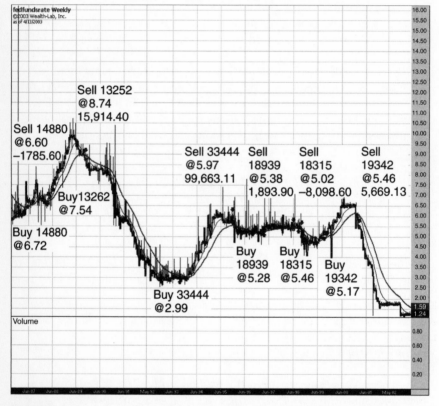

FIGURE 7.7   Federal fund rate, weekly chart from June 1987 to April 2003.

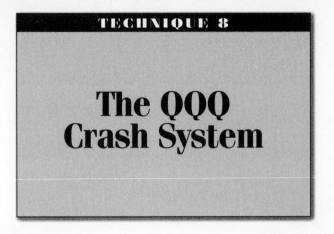

The QQQ Crash System

The QQQs are my asset of choice. Representing the Nasdaq 100 index, the QQQs contain many of the stocks that tend to be valued more on future growth potential than on consistent earnings over the prior 20 years. This method of valuation is what creates the volatility in this index—since nobody really knows how to value its components. When the QQQs move quickly down, a buying opportunity presents itself.

The crash is a close in the QQQs that is 1.5 standard deviations down from its 10-day moving average (use Bollinger bands [see Technique 5] with the 10-day moving average and 1.5 standard deviations to calculate). Using the 10-day average guarantees that the move will be sharp. Using 1.5 standard deviations guarantees that the move is larger than 90 percent of the moves the QQQ has made in its 4-year history.

Here are the rules for using the QQQ crash system:

- Buy the morning after the crash. The dust has settled, the panic is over.
- Sell on the earlier of a close higher than the entry price of the position, or after 20 days (one month).

EXAMPLES

QQQ, 1/22/03

On January 21, 2003, the QQQs closed below 1.5 standard deviations off of the 10-day moving average (the thick line in Figure 8.1). Buying at the open

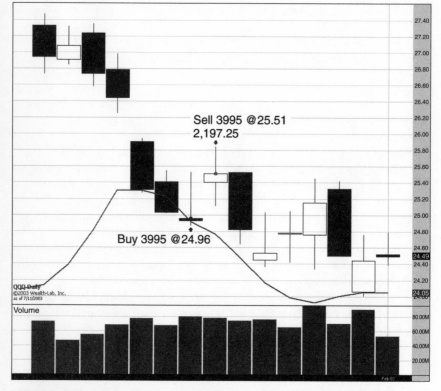

FIGURE 8.1   QQQ on January 22, 2003.

on January 22 at 24.96 and holding for the first up close has the system selling on January 23 at 25.51, for a 2.20 percent profit.

QQQ, 9/18/01

On September 17, 2001, of course, the market tanked, and the QQQs closed below the lower Bollinger band. Holding until the first day the position is profitable (or for 20 days if it is never profitable) has the system holding until October 5, where the system sells at 31.76 for a 0.75 percent profit.

Even though the pressure is on that whole week, and the QQQs keep going down, the snapback is fierce once it happens.

See the results in Table 8.1. Not bad—40 out of 40 successful trades. Whenever I see something like that I have to question the validity of the system. Did the system designer "curve fit," that is, fit the variables to the problem so as to generate a perfect success rate? The three variables in this equation are the size of the moving average (10), the number of standard deviations (1.5), and the length of time I hold the trade if it is not profitable (20).

TABLE 8.1 Results of Basic QQQ Crash

	All Trades
All Trades	40
Average Profit/Loss %	2.55%
Average Bars Held	1.85
Winning Trades	40 (100.00%)
Average Profit %	2.55%
Average Bars Held	1.85
Maximum Consecutive Winning Trades	40
Losing Trades	0 (0.00%)
Average Bars Held	0
Maximum Consecutive Losing Trades	0

Vary the Moving Average

When I used the 20-day moving average, the results were 39 out of 41 successful trades. When I used the 200-day moving average, the results were 30 out of 33 successful trades. A few more variations and the results always seemed to be successful at the 90 percent level or above. So although the results were different than the perfect success record of the 10-day moving average, they were not remarkably different.

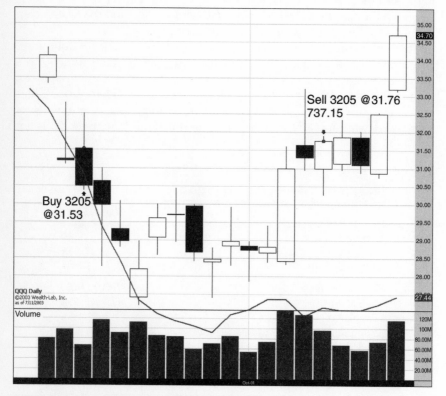

FIGURE 8.2   QQQ on September 18, 2001.

Vary the Standard Deviations

If I used 1 standard deviation instead of 1.5, the results were 71 successful trades out of 74. Note that 1 standard deviation only implies that the move in the QQQs is larger than approximately 66 percent of its historical moves off of its 10-day moving average. Ninety-five percent is more standard and I will stick with it.

Vary the Holding Period

When I varied the holding period lower, the results were again similar. A 10-day holding period resulted in 39 out of 40 successful trades. A 5-day holding period resulted in 37 out of 40 successful trades. So the basic idea holds—when the QQQs suffer a sharp and significant loss, buying is almost always successful.

SIMULATION OF THE BASIC QQQ CRASH SYSTEM

Looking at the results a bit further, assume a 100 percent of equity for each of the 40 trades as shown in Table 8.1. The annual returns are shown in Table 8.2 and Figure 8.3.

I like to look at the maximum adverse excursion for each trade, that is, how much a trade has been unprofitable (i.e., the size of the drawdown) before returning to profitability. The results are summarized in Figure 8.4 (see page 103). The figure shows that out of the 40 profitable trades, 1 went as far as 12 percent down before returning to profitability, with the bulk of the trades not going more than 4 percent down before becoming profitable. For the risk-averse investor, this suggests a possible stop at the 4 or 5 percent level.

Analyzing the drawdowns a bit further as shown in Figure 8.5 (see page 104), we can see that only during the post-9/11 period did the drawdowns get past 8 percent. Now look at Table 8.3, page 105.

TABLE 8.2   Annual Returns

Period Starting	% Return	% Maximum DD	Exposure	Entries	Exits
3/10/1999	6.83	−2.99	0.18	5	5
1/3/2000	60.46	−5.69	5.48	12	12
1/2/2001	10.46	−10.17	5.54	8	8
1/2/2002	32.65	−4.32	3.52	13	13
1/2/2003	2.13	−0.11	1.18	2	2

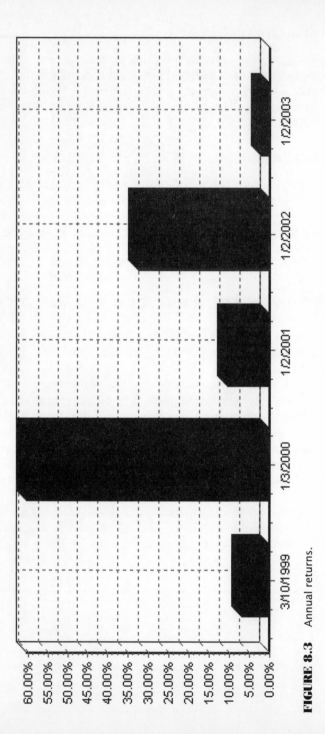

FIGURE 8.3   Annual returns.

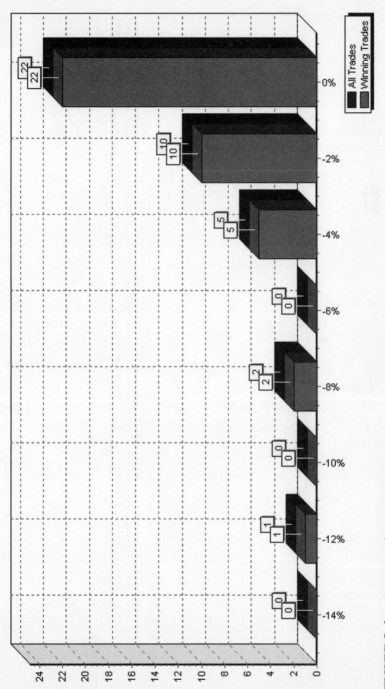

FIGURE 8.4 Maximum adverse excursion.

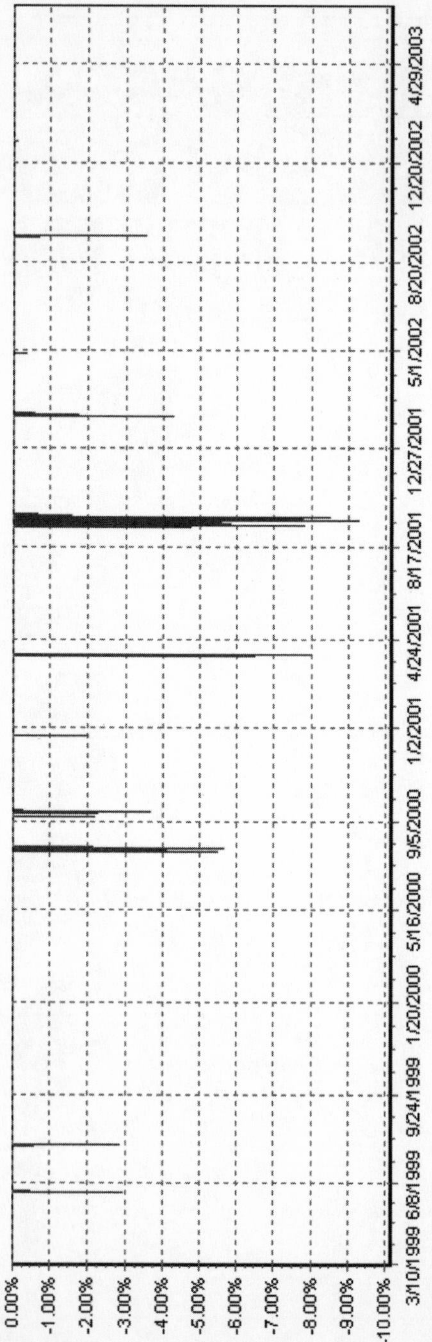

FIGURE 8.5 Underwater equity curve (drawdown).

TABLE 8.3 Trades Using QQQ

Symbol	Entry Date	Entry Price	Exit Date	Exit Price	% Change	Bars Held	MAE %
QQQ	4/20/1999	49.31	4/20/1999	50.65	2.72	1	−0.93
QQQ	5/25/1999	51.47	5/28/1999	52.03	1.09	3	−4.92
QQQ	7/23/1999	57.62	7/28/1999	58.12	0.87	3	−3.19
QQQ	8/5/1999	55.06	8/5/1999	55.93	1.58	1	−2.38
QQQ	9/24/1999	59.62	9/24/1999	60.08	0.77	1	−1.68
QQQ	1/7/2000	82.94	1/7/2000	90	8.51	1	−0.53
QQQ	1/31/2000	85.88	1/31/2000	89.69	4.44	1	−2.77
QQQ	4/17/2000	78.02	4/17/2000	89.62	14.87	1	−0.03
QQQ	5/11/2000	82.75	5/11/2000	84.62	2.26	1	−2.27
QQQ	5/24/2000	75	5/24/2000	79.5	6	1	−3.67
QQQ	7/28/2000	92.19	8/7/2000	92.25	0.07	6	−9.63
QQQ	9/12/2000	93.5	9/20/2000	94.62	1.2	6	−5.88
QQQ	10/4/2000	83.5	10/4/2000	85.62	2.54	1	−1.65
QQQ	11/13/2000	70.95	11/13/2000	71.86	1.28	1	−3.78
QQQ	11/24/2000	68.37	11/24/2000	70.44	3.03	1	−0.29
QQQ	11/30/2000	61.75	11/30/2000	62.98	1.99	1	−2.02
QQQ	12/20/2000	57.31	12/22/2000	60.5	5.57	2	−5.34
QQQ	2/12/2001	56.25	2/12/2001	57.08	1.48	1	−1.12
QQQ	3/13/2001	42.78	3/13/2001	44.45	3.9	1	−1.52
QQQ	4/3/2001	37.2	4/5/2001	37.31	0.3	2	−9.68
QQQ	6/15/2001	41.8	6/15/2001	42.6	1.91	1	−1.24
QQQ	7/11/2001	40.42	7/11/2001	41	1.43	1	−1.36
QQQ	8/22/2001	37.45	8/22/2001	37.69	0.64	1	−2.43
QQQ	9/18/2001	31.53	10/5/2001	31.76	0.73	13	−13.73
QQQ	12/21/2001	39.42	12/21/2001	39.48	0.15	1	−0.68
QQQ	1/17/2002	39.48	1/17/2002	39.65	0.43	1	−1.19
QQQ	1/23/2002	37.65	1/23/2002	38.43	2.07	1	−0.8
QQQ	2/6/2002	36.84	2/13/2002	36.95	0.3	5	−5.08
QQQ	2/22/2002	33.61	2/22/2002	33.65	0.12	1	−1.55
QQQ	3/21/2002	36.15	3/21/2002	37.02	2.41	1	−0.69
QQQ	3/26/2002	35.42	3/26/2002	35.89	1.33	1	−0.06
QQQ	4/29/2002	31.24	4/30/2002	31.73	1.57	1	−2.18
QQQ	5/7/2002	29.27	5/8/2002	31.77	8.54	1	−2.9
QQQ	6/4/2002	28.75	6/4/2002	29.36	2.12	1	−0.49
QQQ	7/24/2002	21.81	7/24/2002	23.62	8.3	1	−0.78
QQQ	9/20/2002	21.83	9/25/2002	21.87	0.18	3	−5.41
QQQ	12/6/2002	25.81	12/6/2002	26.47	2.56	1	−0.27
QQQ	12/10/2002	25.42	12/10/2002	25.6	0.71	1	−0.28
QQQ	1/22/2003	24.96	1/23/2003	25.51	2.2	1	−0.36
QQQ	4/1/2003	25.44	4/1/2003	25.45	0.04	1	−0.75

THE SYSTEM APPLIED TO STOCKS

In Technique 5 on Bollinger bands we can see how a similar system, when used on stocks, results in a high probability of successful profitable trades. However, in this section we see what happens when the QQQs hit their lower Bollinger band, but we buy the components of the QQQs instead of the QQQs themselves.

QQQ-Crash-Stocks #1

- Buy stock X the morning after QQQ falls 1.5 standard deviations below its 10-day moving average.
- Sell at the earlier of stock X closing above the entry price *or* after 20 days go by.

Example: AMZN, 9/18/01   We saw in the previous section what happened when QQQ fell below 1.5 standard deviations off its 10-day moving average on September 17, 2001. The trade, while profitable several days later, was not a huge success. However, if you bought the higher beta components of the QQQ on September 18 rather than the QQQs themselves, the results would have been better (see Figure 8.6). For instance, buying AMZN on the morning of September 18 at 7.59, you would have suffered a decent size drawdown, but 17 days later you would have been able to sell for a 3.4 percent profit at 7.85 on October 11.

Example: BRCM, 1/22/03:   Similar to the AMZN example, buying BRCM on January 22, 2003, at 17.05 instead of buying QQQ would have resulted in a 3.28 percent profit by selling at 17.61 the next day, January 23 (see Figure 8.7, page 109).

The results shown in Table 8.4 (see page 109) do not take into account slippage, which could be huge depending on the liquidity of the stock. But the general principle is confirmed—when the market falls fast, buy high beta stocks.

QQQ-Crash-Stocks #2

Using 1 standard deviation instead of 1.5 standard deviations, on stocks, we get the following system and results:

- Buy stock X the morning after QQQ falls 1 standard deviation below its 10-day moving average.

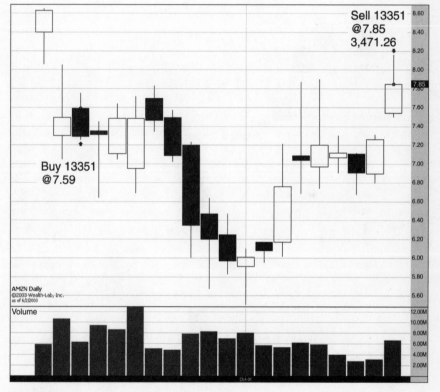

Sell 13351
@7.85
3,471.26

Buy 13351
@7.59

AMZN Daily
©2003 Wealth-Lab, Inc.
as of 6/2/2003

Volume

FIGURE 8.6   AMZN on September 18, 2001.

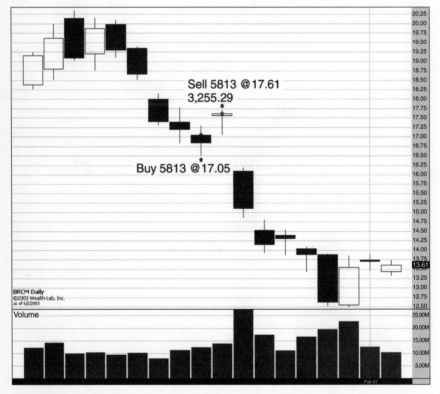

FIGURE 8.7   BRCM on January 21, 2003.

TABLE 8.4 QQQ Crash-Stocks #1

	All Trades
All Trades	3,905
Average Profit/Loss %	2.77%
Average Bars Held	3.04
Winning Trades	3716 (95.16%)
Average Profit %	3.70%
Average Bars Held	2.13
Maximum Consecutive Winning Trades	123
Losing Trades	189 (4.84%)
Average Loss %	−15.48%
Average Bars Held	20.85
Maximum Consecutive Losing Trades	3

- Sell at the earlier of stock X closing above the entry price *or* after 20 days go by.

See Table 8.5 for the results of using 1 standard deviation instead of 1.5.

TABLE 8.5 QQQ Crash-Stocks #2

	All Trades
All Trades	6,984
Average Profit/Loss %	1.70%
Average Bars Held	3.56
Winning Trades	6459 (92.48%)
Average Profit %	3.25%
Average Bars Held	2.14
Maximum Consecutive Winning Trades	169
Losing Trades	525 (7.52%)
Average Loss %	−17.47%
Average Bars Held	20
Maximum Consecutive Losing Trades	4

The Relative Fed Model (and Other Fun Things You Can Do with Yields)

The smart investor pays close attention to what is happening in the bond arena, and in this technique we look at three examples that explain why. First, the idea that bonds compete with stocks for investment value gives rise to variations on the Fed Model, such as my own proprietary Fed Model called the "Relative Fed Model." Second, fast moves in yields often suggest a massive allocation trade is taking place among huge funds, and this allocation may suggest a possible trade in stocks. And, finally, bond investors know what they are talking about at cocktail parties and equity investors are often clueless. So pay attention!

The Fed Model is commonly used to describe a valuation technique whereby you look at Treasury note yields and earnings yields of the S&P 500 and see which one is lower. If earnings yields are lower, then the market is overvalued (i.e., you can make more money investing in T-notes rather than buying the entire S&P 500 for cash and living off the earnings). If earnings yields are higher, then stocks are undervalued. There are many variations on this model. For instance, should you use trailing earnings or forward earnings projections? Forward earnings are really more important; how many of us know the future, let alone the analysts making these projections?

You might wonder, why is this model relevant at all? Stocks are not bonds. Bonds have yields that remain static once purchased (for the most part). In contrast, throughout U.S. history, earnings yields have grown overall.

The Fed model is useful to us only if it can be used somehow to develop a trading vehicle. As it is, it cannot be used that way. If you look at trailing 12-month earnings yields of the S&P 500 vis-à-vis the 10-year Treasury yield, then the number of occurrences in which the 12-month trailing earnings yield is below the 10-year is so infrequent that it is also impossible to test.

Clearly though, there is a relationship between these two yields. Rather than looking at whether one yield is less than the other, look at the spread between the yields. That spread is more a function of sentiment about the future of the economy than anything else, and it does seem to have some bearing on timing the market.

I plotted the earnings yield (trailing 12-month core earnings) of the S&P 500 back to 1982 and did the same for the 10-year T-note. Then I divided the bond yield by the earnings yield and bought the stock market whenever the ratio hit 1.5 standard deviations below its 10-day moving average. Given that the yields are correlated, I am simply buying the market when bond yields tank faster than earnings yields (or earnings yields go up faster than bond yields), regardless of whether one is above the other. I am then selling the market when the ratio gets back to its 10-day moving average.

In summary, 14 trades were made and 10 were profitable (71 percent success rate). The average gain per trade was 11 percent. The current open trade is down 2.1 percent. To make this examination more thorough, I would have to test back further than 1980, but it is a start. The overall point, it seems, is that relative difference is of more interest than static difference between the yields, contrary to what the Fed Model suggests. (See Table 9.1 and Table 9.2.)

TABLE 9.1 Trades Executed (based on extreme shifts in Fed Model)

Entry Date	Price	Exit Date	Exit Price	% Change
2/1/1984	163.41	6/1/1984	150.55	−7.87
7/2/1984	153.16	3/1/1985	181.18	18.29
3/3/1986	226.92	6/2/1986	246.04	8.43
8/1/1986	236.12	10/1/1986	231.32	−2.03
12/1/1987	230.32	3/1/1989	288.86	25.42
7/3/1989	317.98	9/1/1989	351.45	10.53
10/1/1990	306.1	3/1/1991	367.07	19.92

TABLE 9.2 Trades Executed (based on extreme shifts in Fed Model)

Entry Date	Price	Exit Date	Exit Price	% Change
9/1/1992	414.03	3/1/1994	467.19	12.84
12/1/1994	453.55	2/1/1996	636.02	40.23
11/1/1996	705.27	1/2/1997	740.74	5.03
9/1/1998	957.28	1/4/1999	1,229.23	28.41
3/1/2000	1,366.42	5/1/2000	1,452.43	6.29
8/1/2000	1,430.83	6/1/2001	1,255.82	−12.23
8/1/2002	911.62	Open	Open	−2.1

THE BOND ALLOCATION TRADE

When people are in a panic about the state of the world and the economy, it is often the case that both bond yields and stocks fall. Stocks drop for the obvious reasons: If the economy falters, earnings will falter and stocks will underperform. Bonds drop for two reasons: (1) People assume that the Federal Reserve will cut rates in order to juice the economy a bit and (2) funds are fleeing stocks and going into safer bonds.

This panic is a situation that cannot last, however, for two reasons (at least):

1. As yields drop, the discounted back cash flows of corporate America get less discounted, that is, the intrinsic values of companies go up, making them more compatible to the tastes of fundamentally minded investors.

2. As stocks go up and bonds go down (because yields are going up), the allocations in multibillion-dollar pension funds get away from the allocation ranges these funds have set for themselves. In other words, it will suddenly be the case that pension funds find themselves with too large an allocation of bonds and not enough stocks. They have already determined the level of risk and exposure they are willing to take in each category and if that level is exceeded they need to reallocate. Hence, money flows out of bonds and into stocks.

Bond Allocation System

- Buy when the 10-year yield is 25 basis points lower than it was one month prior and when the Dow is down 2 percent in the past week.
- Sell one month later.

See the results in Table 9.3. As shown, there is 75 percent success with 3 percent average return per trade, which compares favorably with an average monthly return of about 0.7 percent on the Dow since 1990.

To up the odds a little bit you can wait for those occasions where yields are down 50 basis points over a one-month period. Then the results are 11 out of 11 successful trades with an average return of 7.12 percent per trade. The trades that resulted from that variation of the system are shown in Table 9.4.

Bond allocation does occur at extremes in both stock market fear and bond market fear. Front running those allocations can be achieved by paying attention to the changes in both markets.

TABLE 9.3   Bond Allocation System (Dow, 1990–2002)

	All Trades
All Trades	95
Average Profit/Loss %	3.09%
Average Bars Held	20
Winning Trades	71 (74.74%)
Average Profit %	6.28%
Average Bars Held	20
Maximum Consecutive Winning Trades	27
Losing Trades	24 (25.26%)
Average Loss %	−6.36%
Average Bars Held	20
Maximum Consecutive Losing Trades	7

TABLE 9.4   Results

Position	Symbol	Entry Date	Entry Price	Exit Date	Exit Price	% Change
Long	^DJI	8/20/1991	2,913.70	9/18/1991	3,017.90	3.58
Long	^DJI	9/22/1998	7,897.20	10/20/1998	8,505.90	7.71
Long	^DJI	10/1/1998	7,632.50	10/29/1998	8,495.00	11.3
Long	^DJI	10/2/1998	7,784.70	10/30/1998	8,592.10	10.37
Long	^DJI	10/5/1998	7,726.20	11/2/1998	8,706.20	12.68
Long	^DJI	12/20/2000	10,318.90	1/22/2001	10,578.20	2.51
Long	^DJI	8/2/2002	8,313.10	8/30/2002	8,663.50	4.22
Long	^DJI	8/5/2002	8,043.60	9/3/2002	8,308.05	3.29
Long	^DJI	9/20/2002	7,986.02	10/18/2002	8,322.40	4.21
Long	^DJI	9/23/2002	7,872.15	10/21/2002	8,538.24	8.46
Long	^DJI	9/24/2002	7,683.13	10/22/2002	8,450.16	9.98

DON'T THROW OUT THE JUNK

Perhaps more predictive than looking at 10-year yields is looking at the junk bond market. When banks and funds are eager to lend money to companies rated as junk, then that activity is potentially a sign that corporate America is doing well. Junk investors spend more time looking over the businesses they lend to—their balance sheets, their quarterly filings, and so forth—than the typical day trader or even mutual fund manager spends on the companies they buy.

When banks are eager to lend, the yields go down and the junk bonds go up. The question is: What happens if junk bonds are going up and the stock market is going down? Is there a potential trade (albeit longer time) that might result?

The Junk System

- Buy the market at the end of a month where the S&P has underperformed the Merrill Lynch High Yield Index by 5 percentage points over the prior three months.
- Sell one month later.

As shown in Table 9.5 an average return of 2.03 percent for a monthly trade compares favorably with the average monthly return of 0.68 percent on the S&P 500 since 1990. Now see Table 9.6 for the trades.

TABLE 9.5 Results, S&P 500 since January 1, 1990

	All Trades
All Trades	28
Average Profit/Loss %	2.03%
Average Bars Held	1
Winning Trades	21 (75.00%)
Average Profit %	4.21%
Average Bars Held	1
Maximum Consecutive Winning Trades	6
Losing Trades	7 (25.00%)
Average Loss %	−4.50%
Average Bars Held	1
Maximum Consecutive Losing Trades	2

TABLE 9.6 Trades on S&P 500 Using the Junk System

Position	Symbol	Entry Date	Entry Price	Exit Date	Exit Price	% Change	MAE %	MFE %
Long	^SPX	10/1/1990	306.1	11/1/1990	304	-0.69	-3.79	4.44
Long	^SPX	11/1/1990	303.99	12/1/1990	322.22	6	-0.78	6.26
Long	^SPX	6/3/1991	389.81	7/1/1991	371.16	-4.78	-5.6	0
Long	^SPX	8/1/1991	387.81	9/1/1991	395.43	1.96	-3.54	2.32
Long	^SPX	10/1/1991	387.86	11/1/1991	392.45	1.18	-3.03	1.53
Long	^SPX	12/2/1991	375.11	1/2/1992	417.09	11.19	-1	11.52
Long	^SPX	1/2/1992	417.03	2/1/1992	408.78	-1.98	-2.01	1
Long	^SPX	5/1/1992	414.95	6/1/1992	415.35	0.1	-1.23	0.92
Long	^SPX	12/1/1997	955.4	1/1/1998	970.43	1.57	-3.19	3.23
Long	^SPX	10/1/1998	1,017.01	11/1/1998	1,098.67	8.03	-9.21	8.53
Long	^SPX	11/2/1998	1,098.67	12/2/1998	1,163.63	5.91	0	8.58
Long	^SPX	11/1/1999	1,362.93	12/1/1999	1,388.91	1.91	-1.21	4.58
Long	^SPX	1/2/2001	1,320.28	2/2/2001	1,366.01	3.46	-3.46	4.78
Long	^SPX	3/1/2001	1,239.94	4/1/2001	1,160.33	-6.42	-12.8	2.22
Long	^SPX	4/2/2001	1,160.33	5/2/2001	1,249.46	7.68	-5.89	9.39
Long	^SPX	5/1/2001	1,249.46	6/1/2001	1,255.82	0.51	-1.4	5.32
Long	^SPX	6/1/2001	1,255.82	7/1/2001	1,224.38	-2.5	-4.2	2.45
Long	^SPX	10/1/2001	1,040.94	11/1/2001	1,059.78	1.81	-1.36	6.69
Long	^SPX	11/1/2001	1,059.78	12/1/2001	1,139.45	7.52	-0.52	9.78
Long	^SPX	12/3/2001	1,139.45	1/3/2002	1,148.08	0.76	-2.19	3
Long	^SPX	6/3/2002	1,067.14	7/1/2002	989.82	-7.25	-10.7	0.34
Long	^SPX	7/1/2002	989.82	8/1/2002	911.62	-7.9	-21.63	0.47
Long	^SPX	8/1/2002	911.62	9/1/2002	916.07	0.49	-8.58	5.86
Long	^SPX	10/1/2002	815.28	11/1/2002	885.76	8.64	-5.72	11.3
Long	^SPX	11/1/2002	885.76	12/1/2002	936.31	5.71	-1.55	6.33
Long	^SPX	3/3/2003	841.15	4/1/2003	848.18	0.84	-6.21	6.51
Long	^SPX	4/1/2003	848.18	5/1/2003	916.92	8.1	-0.04	8.97
Long	^SPX	5/1/2003	916.92	6/1/2003	963.59	5.09	-1.54	5.29

CONCLUSION

Most stock investors do not look at bonds at all and I think this is a mistake. For one thing, bonds are actually a pretty good trading vehicle if you do not mind the leverage. For another, bonds are the primary alternative to large asset allocaters such as state pension funds. If bonds are making a huge run in either direction, it could be that an asset allocation trade is about to take place and you should be aware. Finally, bond investors are, on the whole, usually somewhat more aware of company issues, economic issues, and global macro issues than the average investor. Following their lead is often a profitable way to make money for us folks who often find ourselves counted with the dumb money.

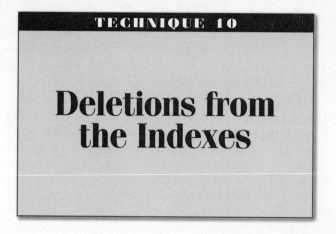

TECHNIQUE 10

Deletions from the Indexes

The market is fairly efficient and absorbs new information quickly. When a company announces bad earnings, the stock usually falls fast, too fast to take advantage of the new information by shorting. When a company announces it is going to be bought, arbitrage funds instantly start buying up the shares, propelling it to the merger price sometimes within seconds. One case where the market retains a pocket of inefficiency is when it comes to the addition and deletion of stocks into the various indexes that track the broader market.

Index funds have become increasingly popular ever since 1976 when John Bogle proposed to the Vanguard Group that it create the first index fund to track the S&P 500. His goals seemed unambitious at the time—all he wanted to do was to perform as well as the S&P 500. Not pick stocks that would outperform, not try any fancy growth or value strategies. Just simply keep pace with the index. Since then index funds that track all of the relevant S&P indexes, Russell indexes, Nasdaq 100, Wilshire 5000, and so on have sprung up, and these funds have outperformed approximately 80 percent of the actively managed mutual funds out there. The largest period of growth occurred in the 1990s when the S&P 500 increased at an annual rate of 17.4 percent. In the 1990s we also saw the advent of the ETFs, such as SPY and QQQ, that allow investors to invest in (and, of course, day trade) funds that track the S&P 500 and Nasdaq 100, respectively. The amount of money in index funds is in the hundreds of billions of dollars, and any small change in the indexes effects the flow of that money.

A common strategy that many people play is to buy a stock after the S&P announces that it is going to be added to one of its indexes. Index funds are typically not buying on the announcement (since it is not in the index until the "effective date," which could be several weeks later). It is a guarantee that they will be buying the stock, so individual investors and actively managed funds can begin buying ahead of the announcement. In the paper "Investor Awareness and Market Segmentation: Evidence from S&P 500 Changes," the authors, Honghui Chen of the University of Baltimore, Gregory Noronha of Arizona State University West, and Vijay Singal of Virginia Tech, analyze the effect of index changes prior to the effective date. They conclude that, on average, between the announcement date and the effective date, a stock tends to rise about 5 percent. Deleted stocks, they say, do not fall as much, the reason being that part of the new buyers of added stocks are investors who have become newly aware of the stock because of the addition. Investors do not suddenly become aware of the deleted stocks, so the effect is less pronounced going into the effective date although they do note that there is some selloff.

My favorite example of a stock running up into the addition date was JDSU, which was added to the S&P 500 on July 26, 2000. Many people considered JDSU to potentially be the next MSFT, a stock with almost infinite promise and growth potential. Telecom was booming and everyone assumed that the telecom companies would have to buy enough fiber and components to put fiber directly going into your home. The demand was thought to be extreme and would last for years. In the months prior to the addition, posts on the Yahoo! message board for JDSU like the following were quite common:

> *What I do to make money is buy and hold QCOM and JDSU (and others) . . . when they pull back I play options. When JDSU pulled back from 273 to 210 a few weeks ago, I bought a ton of MAR250 and MAR280 calls . . . I sold some of these the other day for a +250% profit and bought more JDSU shares for long term with the profits . . . and today I bought more. Like I said before, I don't care if JDSU follows the entire market down, over the long term it will far outperform the overall market. By the split in March, I guarantee we'll be well over 200. This is how to make money.*

Figure 10.1 shows JDSU for the months of July and August, 2000. This is a classic example of a stock that ran up, in this case more than 40 percent on high volume as speculators and index funds started buying up the shares, in the three weeks before addition, culminating in the stock hitting an all-time high of 140.50 on the effective date of the addition. Buyers of S&P 500 funds never had it so good again as JDSU began a nonstop fall at that very point, never hitting 140 again. Within one year, the stock was in single digits and at the time of this writing, JDSU is at 3.58.

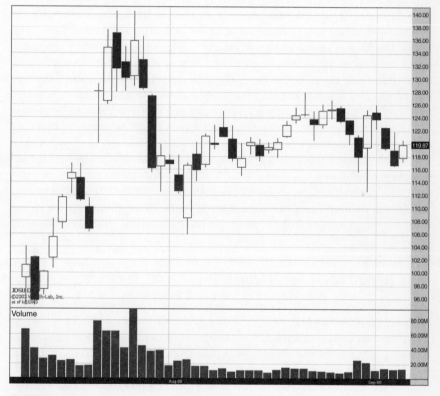

FIGURE 10.1 JDSU for July–August 2000.

Is this a strategy that is still playable? To be honest, I don't know. I have not studied or even considered studying it. Too many people are looking into this idea, so even if this strategy works now, it will not work in the future. Web sites and services have sprung up to predict the most likely to be added to an index so people can start buying even before the announcement date. Also, index funds have been improving their strategies for buying up shares, further nullifying the effect. It is not an interesting strategy to me.

However, the subject of deletions and what happens to them is an interesting and, I think, playable strategy. A stock is deleted from an index for many reasons: the price has gotten too low, earnings have gone down, liquidity has dried up, the company went bankrupt or was merged, or the stock might have been promoted to another index (e.g., from small cap to mid cap). Going into the effective date, again, many people are playing the strategy of shorting the stock until the effective date. Also, in addition to index funds selling the stock, many actively managed funds might also be selling the stock. Despite being actively managed, they might be required by charter to only invest in stocks that are members of a select group of indexes.

In other words, there is a heavy amount of irrational selling that is taking place having nothing to do with the basic information flows about the company. Opportunity must be lurking somewhere when this happens!

EXAMPLES

ORB, October–November 2001

Figure 10.2 shows the chart for Orbital Sciences, ORB, for October and November 2001. On November 2, 2001, the stock was scheduled to be deleted from the S&P 600. Through the month of October, the stock was sliding, touching a low of almost 20 percent lower from the beginning of the month to mid-October. On November 2, it was deleted and then began an incredible rise from 2.1 to 3.21, 13 days later—a gain of greater than 50 percent. No serious news about the company was coming out. On the Yahoo! message boards investors were completely perplexed. Nobody had any idea what would make the stock go up 50 percent. Sixty trading days after the effective date of the deletion from the index, the stock was at 5.40.

FIGURE 10.2   ORB for October–November 2001.

FTUS, Mid-September to Mid-November 2002

Figure 10.3 (see page 125) shows the chart for FTUS from mid-September, 2002, to mid-November, 2002. The stock was deleted from the S&P 600 index on October 11, 2002. In the month leading up to the deletion date, the stock was down almost every single day, going from a high of 2.80 to 1.26 the day it was deleted from the index. Thirteen trading days later the stock was at 1.55, a gain of over 20 percent. Then, on November 8, a random buy recommendation on an obscure Web site sent the stock into a short squeeze frenzy. It opened that day at 2.40 and closed at 4.45. Again, no news. Just pent-up selling into the index deletion that created a short squeeze condition.

WHX, September 15 to November 21, 2000

Figure 10.4 (see page 126) goes from September 15, 2000, to November 21, 2000. WHX was deleted from the S&P 600 index on the 26th of September. The selling and volume increase drastically right before the deletion date. On the 25th, the day before the deletion date, the stock opened at 7.50 and then promptly hit a 52-week low at 3.38 before closing at 4.12. It took 5 days after the deletion date for the stock to make its way back to 7.50. Twenty days after deletion the stock was at 6.00. Currently, 3 years after the deletion from the index, the stock is sitting in the 2s.

A STUDY OF THE DATA

Charles Kornblith, an undergraduate student at Wharton University, has done an excellent study on the effects of deletions on the S&P 600 index, the results of which are presented here with his permission. Why the S&P 600 index? There can be no more beaten down, humiliated stock than the dregs that are kicked out of the S&P 600 Small Cap index. These stocks are usually being kicked out with no other home to go to, and, in many cases, are on their way to the over-the-counter (OTC) boards or worse. Nevertheless, the snapback after a deletion in these stocks is often extraordinary.

As one can see from Table 10.1 through Table 10.8 (see pages 127–132), the average return from 1997 to 2002 per stock deleted from the S&P 600 was 7.94 percent the day after deletion and 15.84 percent within 10 days after deletion. Is this a playable strategy? It might be. While the price performance has been very good for these stocks the problem is, as Kornblith mentioned to me in his e-mail documenting the study, the illiquidity of some of these stocks plus the low prices could cause much slippage and commissions pain.

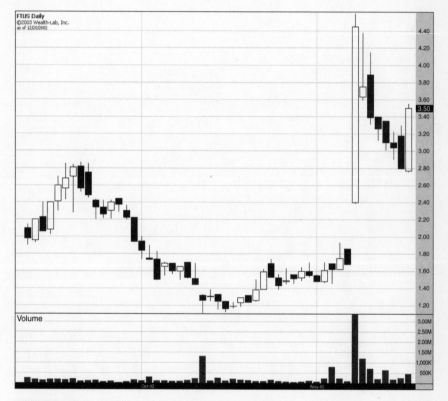

FIGURE 10.3 FTUS from mid-September to mid-November 2002.

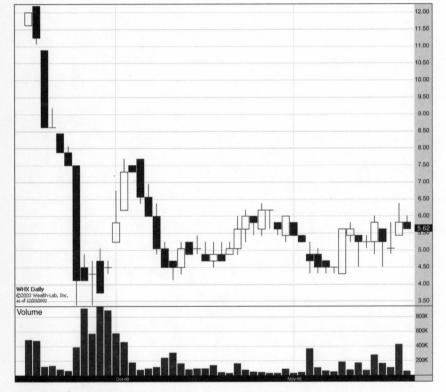

FIGURE 10.4   WHX from September 15 to November 21, 2000.

TABLE 10.1 Stocks Deleted from the S&P 600 from 1997–2002, with Returns the Day of the Deletion (T), 10 Days After, and 20 Days After

	Ticker	Date Effective	T = 0	T = 10	T = 20
Titan International	TWI	12/6/2002	1.35	1.38	1.4
Trenwick Group	TWK	11/14/2002	4.3	2.67	1.05
Aspen Technology	AZPN	10/11/2002	0.801	1.5	1.88
Factory 2-U Stores	FTUS	10/11/2002	1.26	1.43	4.46
AXT Inc.	AXTI	10/11/2002	1	1.13	1.75
Electroglas, Inc.	EGLS	10/11/2002	1.23	1.44	2.339
Franklin Covey	FC	9/30/2002	1.18	1.19	1.49
EPresence Inc.	EPRE	9/30/2002	problem with data		
Stratex Networks Inc.	STXN	9/30/2002	1.279	1.09	1.75
Therma-Wave Inc.	TWAV	9/30/2002	0.79	0.39	0.58
Cygnus Inc.	CYGN	8/15/2002	0.729	1.52	1.51
Aspect Communications	ASPT	7/24/2002	1.3	1.42	1.71
InterVoice	INTV	7/11/2002	1.01	1.63	1.74
Penton Media Publishing	PME	7/11/2002	1	0.3	0.52
Read-Rite Corp.	RDRT	6/28/2002	0.48	0.53	0.33
Seitel, Inc.	SEI	6/12/2002	1.11	1.09	0.72
Valence Technology	VLNC	6/12/2002	1.42	1.37	1.25
Advanced Tissue Sciences	ATIS	6/12/2002	1.09	1.16	1.11
Stratos Lightwave, Inc.	STLW	6/12/2002	1.519	1.6	1.03
Mississippi Chemical	GRO	5/1/2002	1.42	1.4	1.4
Visual Networks	VNWK	4/24/2002	1.4	1.45	1.73
SLI Inc.	SLI	4/18/2002	0.94	0.48	0.76
BMC Industries	BMM	3/1/2002	1.44	1.94	1.68
Organogenesis, Inc.	ORG	2/21/2002	1.39	1.43	—
Mutual Risk Management	MM	2/21/2002	1.05	0.96	0.75
Brightpoint Inc.	CELL	2/7/2002	0.66	0.87	1.33
Foster Wheeler Ltd.	FWC	1/16/2002	1.78	2.53	2.56
APW Ltd.	APW	12/31/2001	1.67	0.68	0.35
Amcast Industrial	AIZ	11/30/2001	5	5.32	5.38
Auspex Systems	ASPX	11/30/2001	1.421	1.39	1.8
Tenneco Automotive	TEN	11/15/2001	1.55	1.56	1.67
Orbital Sciences Corp.	ORB	11/2/2001	2.1	3.4	3.58
Mayor's Jewelers Inc.	MYR	10/9/2001	1.02	1.39	—
SpeedFam-IPEC Inc.	SFAM	10/9/2001	1.02	1.4799	2.9
Int'l. FiberCom, Inc.	IFCI	10/9/2001	0.9	0.95	0.79
SONICblue Inc.	SBLU	10/5/2001	0.8	1.05	—
Innovex, Inc.	INVX	10/5/2001	1.34	2	—
Hartmarx Corp.	HMX	8/6/2001	1.95	3.45	3.52
Polaroid Corp.	PRD	7/18/2001	1.2	1.3	1.5
Alliance Pharmaceutica	ALLP	7/18/2001	1.46	1.44	1.74

(continued)

TABLE 10.1   Continued

	Ticker	Date Effective	T = 0	T = 10	T = 20
Pac-West Telecommunica	PACW	7/11/2001	1.15	0.96	0.92
Edgewater Technology	EDGW	7/6/2001	3.35	3.33	3.45
Gottschalks, Inc.	GOT	7/6/2001	3	3.45	3.28
eLoyalty Corporation	ELOY	6/14/2001	1.06	0.99	0.77
Robotic Vision Systems	ROBV	5/31/2001	1.56	1.86	1.84
Lillian Vernon	LVC	5/23/2001	7.13	8.92	8.92
Cyrk Inc.	CYRK	5/11/2001	2.45	0	0
Casual Male Corp.	CMAL	5/11/2001	1.14	0	0
Cone Mills	COE	4/27/2001	1.64	1.45	1.37
Immune Response Corp.	IMNR	4/16/2001	1.48	3.15	5.95
Exabyte Corp.	EXBT	4/2/2001	1.0625	0.99	1.06
P-Com Inc.	PCOM	4/2/2001	1.6562	1.4	1.07
New Century Equity Hld	NCEH	3/30/2001	1.125	1.31	1.28
Damark International	DMRK	3/22/2001	2.71	3.25	3.25
Adaptive Broadband Cor	ADAP	3/22/2001	0.9	0.75	0
Friede Goldman	FGH	3/8/2001	2	2.15	0.98
HA-LO Industries	HMK	3/8/2001	1.3	1.09	0.96
Washington Group Int'l	WNG	3/5/2001	1.07	1.86	1.57
Nashua Corp.	NSH	2/27/2001	3.06	4.9	4.7
Dixie Group Inc.	DXYN	1/31/2001	2.3437	2.625	3.4375
Books-A-Million	BAMM	12/29/2000	1.375	2	2.125
Spartan Motors	SPAR	12/28/2000	1.3437	1.9375	2.6562
Bombay Company	BBA	12/28/2000	1.93	2.37	2.37
Laser Vision Centers	LVCI	12/20/2000	1.1875	1.875	2.0625
Hanger Orthopedic Group	HGR	12/11/2000	1.31	0.93	1.25
Ames Department Stores	AMES	12/11/2000	1.5	1.38	—
Frozen Food Express Ind.	FFEX	12/8/2000	1.25	1.4375	1.6875
Insteel Industries Inc.	III	12/4/2000	1	1.25	3
TALK.Com, Inc.	TALK	11/28/2000	0.57	2	—
Birmingham Steel	BIR	11/16/2000	1.37	1.25	1.37
Chiquita Brands	CQB	11/7/2000	1.5	1.75	1.56
Epicor Software	EPIC	11/2/2000	1	1.1562	1.0312
CKE Restaurants	CKR	10/4/2000	2.44	2	—
Guilford Mills	GFD	10/4/2000	1.31	1.88	—
WHX Corp.	WHX	9/26/2000	4.11	4.5	6
GC Companies	GCX	9/20/2000	3.12	2.93	2.37
Pillowtex Corp.	PTX	8/10/2000	1.25	2.5625	2.375
Lason Inc.	LSON	8/8/2000	1.1875	2.8125	2.125
Oakwood Homes	OH	8/8/2000	1.5	1.62	1.68
Komag Inc.	KMAG	8/2/2000	1.1562	1.4375	2.3125
Coeur d'Alene Mines	CDE	7/27/2000	1.37	1.43	1.37
Swiss Army Brands	SABI	7/27/2000	4.25	4.375	4.1875
Sports Authority	TSA	6/30/2000	1.56	1.62	1.5
Magellan Health Services	MGL	6/23/2000	1.25	1.37	1.62
Inacom Corp.	ICO	5/2/2000	0.9375	1.0625	0

	Ticker	Date Effective	T = 0	T = 10	T = 20
PictureTel Corp.	PCTL	4/19/2000	3.53	4.12	—
Aviation Sales	AVS	4/19/2000	3.75	6.31	6.25
Rural/Metro Corp.	RURL	3/31/2000	1.1875	2	2
Frontier Insurance Group	FTR	3/29/2000	0.93	1.06	0.87
Genesis Health Ventures	GHV	2/23/2000	1.25	1.6875	0.8125
Southern Energy Homes	SEHI	2/15/2000	1.2187	1.3437	1.2187
USA Detergents	USAD	1/28/2000	2.25	2.46	2.31
NCS Healthcare Inc.	NCSS	1/28/2000	1.46875	1.90625	2.34375
AMRESCO Inc.	AMMB	1/13/2000	1.06	1.31	1.31
Benton Oil & Gas	BNO	1/3/2000	1.81	1.88	—
Delta Woodside Ind.	DLW	12/30/1999	1.87	1.93	1.62
Hecla Mining	HL	12/30/1999	1.56	1.5	1.43
PhyCor Inc.	PHYC	11/23/1999	1.15625	1.1875	1.3125
Galey & Lord Inc.	GNL	11/4/1999	1.31	2.68	2.18
Integrated Health Services	IHS	10/21/1999	0.375	0.25	0.3125
Molecular Biosystems	MB	10/1/1999	1.625	1.375	1
Family Golf Centers	FGCI	8/31/1999	1.25	2.875	2.875
Applied Magnetics	APM	8/31/1999	0.9375	1	0.8125
System Software	SSAX	8/30/1999	0.9375	0	0
TCSI Corp.	TCSI	8/30/1999	1.625	1.6875	1.5
Breed Technologies	BDT	8/17/1999	0.4375	0.6875	0.625
Dialogic Corp.	DLGC	7/2/1999	43.9063	0	0
Mariner Post-Acute	MPN	6/18/1999	0.625	0.34375	0.6875
Lechters Inc.	LECH	4/30/1999	1.53	2.21	2.25
Johnston Industries	JII	4/30/1999	1.5	2.5	2.25
LSB Industries	LSB	4/30/1999	2.1875	2	2.0625
Hauser Inc.	HAUS	4/27/1999	1.5	2.5625	2.4375
KCS Energy Inc.	KCS	4/27/1999	1.12	1.37	0.68
Glamis Gold Ltd.	GLG	3/1/1999	1.56	1.68	1.5
Wiser Oil	WZR	12/31/1998	2.12	2.75	2
Shoney's Inc.	SHN	12/31/1998	1.375	1.9375	2.8125
Filene's Basement	BSMT	12/15/1998	1.5	2.09375	3.375
Northwestern	NWSW	12/10/1998	0.8125	0.8125	0.90625
Tultex Corp.	TTX	12/10/1998	0.75	0.8125	0.9375
BroadBand Technologies	BBTK	10/22/1998	1.3125	2.75	2.75
Zoll Medical	ZOLL	5/28/1998	5.8125	6.6875	7.875
Designs, Inc.	DESI	5/14/1998	1.75	1.5	1.8125
ImmuLogic Pharmaceuticals	IMUL	3/30/1998	1.5	1.53125	1.9375
SciClone Pharmaceuticals	SCLN	3/19/1998	3.1875	4.2812	4.0625
National Auto Credit	NAK	3/4/1998	1.75	1.9375	0
Geotek Communications	GOTK	2/9/1998	1.75	0	0
Tseng Labs	TSNG	1/14/1998	1.40625	1.375	1.5
NTN Communications	NTN	12/31/1997	1	1	0.93
CellPro, Inc.	CPRO	10/6/1997	problem with data		
Air & Water Technologies	AWT	9/25/1997	1.75	1.875	1.4375

(*continued*)

TABLE 10.1 Continued

	Ticker	Date Effective	T = 0	T = 10	T = 20
JumboSports, Inc.	JSI	9/2/1997	3.3125	3.9375	3.5
RDM Sports Group	RDM	8/7/1997	0.69	0.5	—
Levitz Furniture	LFI	7/25/1997	1.13	1.5	—
Pharmaceutical Resources	PRX	7/25/1997	2.25	2.06	2.06
Payless Cashways	PCS	7/17/1997	problem with data		
Banyan Systems	BNYN	5/27/1997	1.9375	1.9375	1.875
Casino Magic	CMAG	5/27/1997	1.28125	1.375	1.125
Venture Stores	VEN	5/27/1997	2.5	2.625	2.5
Compression Labs	CLIX	3/31/1997	problem with data		
Omega Environmental	OMEG	3/31/1997	problem with data		
Sunshine Mining	SSC	1/22/1997	6.5	7.5	9
Merisel, Inc.	MSEL	1/13/1997	1.8125	1.9687	1.9375

Source: Courtesy of Charles Kornblith, Wharton University.

TABLE 10.2 Total Study

	T = 1	T = 5	T = 10
Total Return	1079.66%	2010.02%	2154.03%
Number of Samples	136	136	136
Average Return	7.94%	14.78%	15.84%
Standard Deviation	20.10%	29.62%	45.31%
SEM	0.0172	0.0254	0.0388
Z-score	4.6054	5.8185	4.0769

Notes: SEM = stdev/sqrt(N); Z-score = avg. return / SEM.
Source: Courtesy of Charles Kornblith, Wharton University.

TABLE 10.3 2002 Returns Breakdown

	T = 1	T = 5	T = 10
Total Return	82.11%	134.81%	212.76%
Number of Samples	26	26	26
Samples Excluded Due to Problems with Data	1	1	1
Average Return	3.16%	5.19%	8.18%
Standard Deviation	11.36%	27.74%	38.96%
SEM	0.0222755	0.05440983	0.0764065
Z-score	1.4177141	0.95296697	1.0710029

Notes: SEM = stdev/sqrt(N); Z-score = avg. return / SEM.
Source: Courtesy of Charles Kornblith, Wharton University.

TABLE 10.4 2001 Returns Breakdown

	T = 1	T = 5	T = 10
Total Return	140.89%	505.61%	330.38%
Number of Samples	33	33	33
Samples Excluded Due to Problems with Data	0	0	0
Average Return	17.43%	30.71%	44.03%
Standard Deviation	0.0303406	0.05345777	0.0766383
SEM	1.4072023	2.8661064	1.3063482
Z-score			

Notes: SEM = stdev/sqrt(N); Z-score = avg. return / SEM.

TABLE 10.5 2000 Returns Breakdown

	T = 1	T = 5	T = 10
Total Return	546.32%	870.75%	1064.10%
Number of Samples	35	35	35
Samples Excluded Due to Problems with Data	0	0	0
Average Return	15.61%	24.88%	30.40%
Standard Deviation	29.89%	36.44%	50.47%
SEM	0.0505163	0.0615877	0.085302
Z-score	3.0899317	4.03955358	3.5641278

Notes: SEM = stdev/sqrt(N); Z-score = avg. return / SEM.

TABLE 10.6 1999 Returns Breakdown

	T = 1	T = 5	T = 10
Total Return	141.37%	247.80%	313.97%
Number of Samples	18	18	18
Samples Excluded Due to Problems with Data	1	1	1
Average Return	7.85%	13.77%	17.44%
Standard Deviation	19.48%	29.69%	54.86%
SEM	0.0459145	0.06996956	0.1292996
Z-score	1.7105537	1.96752364	1.3490194

Notes: SEM = stdev/sqrt(N); Z-score = avg. return / SEM.

TABLE 10.7 1998 Returns Breakdown

	T = 1	T = 5	T = 10
Total Return	108.25%	169.06%	173.72%
Number of Samples	13	13	13
Samples Excluded Due to Problems with Data	0	0	0
Average Return	8.33%	13.00%	13.36%
Standard Deviation	9.40%	11.66%	46.19%
SEM	0.0260656	0.03232575	0.1281
Z-score	3.1945545	4.02289179	1.043188

Notes: SEM = stdev/sqrt(N); Z-score = avg. return / SEM.

TABLE 10.8 1997 Returns Breakdown

	T = 1	T = 5	T = 10
Total Return	60.71%	81.99%	59.09%
Number of samples	11	11	11
Samples Excluded Due to Problems with Data	4	4	4
Average Return	5.52%	7.45%	5.37%
Standard Deviation	7.52%	8.19%	15.43%
SEM	0.0226698	0.02469881	0.0465221
Z-score	2.4346512	3.01772042	1.1547403

Notes: SEM = stdev/sqrt(N); Z-score = avg. return / SEM.

CONCLUSION

Further avenues of study before using an approach based on deletion from the indexes include:

- What is the effect of deletions on the other indexes? Nasdaq 100 stocks, in particular, have a lot more liquidity and volatility.
- What happens in the Kornblith study when taking into account volume (i.e., only buying the stocks with x shares of volume per day)?
- What happens when you only look at the stocks that had the largest price decreases prior to the effective date?

Nevertheless, despite these concerns, if a direct-access broker is used to keep commissions low, I think a strategy based on deletions from the index is playable.

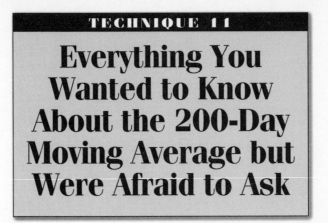

Everything You Wanted to Know About the 200-Day Moving Average but Were Afraid to Ask

Constantly we hear reference to the 200-day moving average in the media. "The S&P index just crossed its 200-day moving average and this is a very bullish sign." "MSFT crossed its moving average so we should expect to see a nice upwards move over the next week." And so on. I was skeptical. It does not seem to make sense to me that this movement would be a bullish event. Plus, most of the time I read or hear about the 200-day moving average, people are talking about the entry (the crossover of the average) but never the exit so it has been hard to formulate a successful trading strategy. Also, I was never sure what people meant by the word "bullish." Does it mean the market goes up forever now? Or just tomorrow?

First of all, what is the 200-day moving average? Simply put, it is the prices of the prior 200 days added together and divided by 200. As can be seen in Figure 11.1, a chart of the 200-day moving average, most of the time when we are in a bull market, the closing daily price of the S&P is above the 200-day moving average, and most of the time when we are in a bear market, the closing price of the S&P 500 is below the 200-day moving average. The real question is, when the daily price of the S&P closes over the 200-day moving average, are we also moving from a bear period to a bull period?

In the following I present several possible systems using the 200-day moving average. First I attempt to mirror and test the prognosticators in the media that forecast the change in trend with each move in the 200-day moving average. Then I demonstrate a long-only system based on the idea of using the 200-day moving average as a *countertrend* indicator that has worked well in both bull and bear markets.

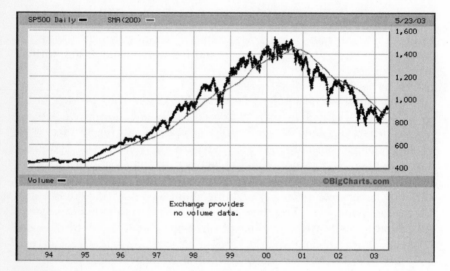

FIGURE 11.1   S&P 200-day moving average.

TRADING SYSTEMS

Here is the system I feel most closely mirrors what the media is forecasting when the 200-day moving average is mentioned:

- Buy the S&P when the close crosses over the 200-day moving average.
- Sell when the S&P crosses below the 200-day moving average.

It is hard to qualify this outlook as bullish, but the results are positive. The reason for the hesitation is that only 28 percent of the occurrences of this system have resulted in a positive trade. In other words, if the S&P closes above its 200-day moving average, then there is a 70 percent chance it will be lower by the time it goes below its 200-day moving average.

That said, doing this trade on every occurrence since 1950 would have made an investor money in the long haul. In summary: of the 142 occurrences since 1950, 40 were successful and 102 were unsuccessful, with an average return per trade of 3.23 percent (including the losses). An amount of $10,000 put into this system in 1950 would be worth $55,000 now; $10,000 put into a buy and hold strategy, however, would now be worth $494,000.

Particularly since January 1, 2000, there have been many false starts to this indicator (Figure 11.2), with 17 occurrences and only 2 successful (including the most recent one that opened on April 21, 2003, and not closed yet). So when someone says "we just crossed over the 200-day moving average so now we are in a bull market," it is best not to believe it.

THE ONE DAY 200 DMA SYSTEM

Here is another system:

- Buy the S&P when the close crosses the 200-day moving average.
- Sell one day later.

The idea is that maybe people get so excited about the event of the crossing that they rush to buy.

The result is mildly positive but not statistically significant and does not beat commissions and slippage. Of the 147 occurrences since 1950, 74 were successful and 73 were unsuccessful, with an average return of 0.11 percent (equivalent to 1 point in the S&P today).

However, the results get a little better when you buy the 200-day crossover and hold for one month: 72% successful with an average gain of 1.65 percent as opposed to the 0.68% average monthly return since 1950.

FIGURE 11.2   False starts.

The last trade in this system started on April 17, 2003, and ended on May 16, for a gain of 5.68 percent. Holding for a quarter does not improve the results: 2.67 percent per trade as opposed to an average quarterly return of 2.04 percent since 1950.

So perhaps it is bullish when the S&P 500 crosses its 200-day moving average and you hold for a month. Basically you can get double the return when compared to a random buy and holding for a month.

What happens now if you run the one month 200 DMA system on a basket of your favorite stocks? Buy a stock when it crosses its 200-day moving average then sell one month later. I ran the test on the stocks in the S&P 400 mid-cap index over the past eight years as a simulation where each trade took up 1 percent of equity. The results were marginally okay: average return of 0.62 percent per trade with the yearly returns shown in Figure 11.3 demonstrating that you would have survived the worst of the bear market but still taken a big hit in 2002.

In general, although conceptually it does seem bullish when the indexes cross their 200-day moving averages, it does not seem like there is a worthwhile trading strategy that results. Therefore, I decided to try one more approach: a contrarian one that depends on the concept of mean reversion, that is, buy when the price of the S&P hits an extreme low relative to its 200-day moving average. Specifically, and simply:

- Buy when the S&P closes 20 percent below its 200-day moving average (e.g., the crash of 1987 or on September 20, 2001)
- Sell one month (20 trading days) later.

Since 1950, utilizing this system results in 79 trades, 65 of which were profitable (82 percent) and 14 unprofitable (17 percent) for an average return of 6.43 percent per trade as opposed to a return of 0.68 percent if one randomly buys any month. Not bad. Interestingly, if one only looks at the data for the S&P 500 index since 1975, this system would have resulted in 34 out of 34 successful trades with an average return of 10 percent per trade. The last trade started on October 10, 2002 and ended on November 7, 2002, returning a nice 12.28 percent. Enough to pay the bills and have a glass of wine to celebrate.

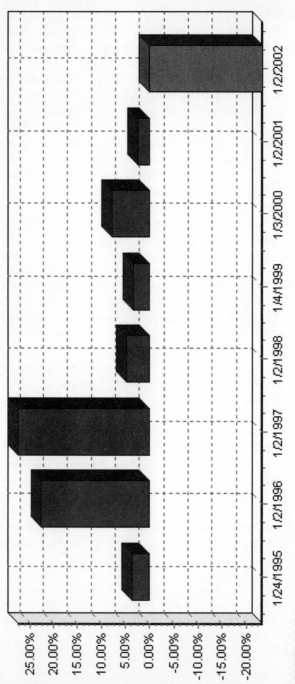

FIGURE 11.3   Annual returns.

CONCLUSION

Arguing about what direction the trend of the market is in (bull or bear) based on the 200-day moving average might be fun at cocktail parties but will not really make anyone money. Instead, buying when the trend is absolutely, unequivocally *down* and the market is plummeting vis-à-vis its 200-day moving average is usually the best time to take a trade on the long side. By the time the talking heads are debating a new trend when the price closes above the 200-day moving average, you are long gone out of the market, hopefully on vacation.

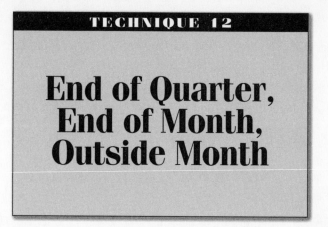

TECHNIQUE 12

End of Quarter, End of Month, Outside Month

THE END OF THE QUARTER MYTH

As I write this, it is June 29, 2003, and tomorrow is the last day of the quarter. On the various systems I play I am getting a pretty strong short signal at the open on Nasdaq futures in the morning. I mentioned this to two different friends of mine—one a stockbroker at Morgan Stanley, the other a professional money manager who manages $500M in assets. Both of them said the same thing, "Oh man, I wouldn't short QQQ the last day of the quarter. Aren't you afraid of end of quarter window dressing?"

I did a search on Google for "End of quarter" and "window dressing" and got 545 results. A typical quote was, "you might want to consider holding it a bit longer than you might otherwise, through the window dressing period. . . ." It does not make sense to me in general. I mean, it is not as if a fund manager is going to improve his returns by marking up stocks like MSFT or INTC. The volume is too great for any mutual fund machinations to have any effect at all.

So I ran a test of an end-of-quarter shorting system:

- Short the open on the last day of the quarter.
- Cover at the end of the day.

I got the following results:

QQQ: 8 out of 16 successful; average return of +0.68 percent.

SMH: 9 out of 11 successful; average return of +1.72 percent.

SPY: 29 out 41 successful; average return of +0.34 percent.

^NDX (since 1988): 24 out of 60 successful; average return of +0.10 percent.

^SPX (since 1988): 33 out of 60 successful; average return of +0.11 percent.

^RUT (since 1987): 10 out of 62 successful; average return of –0.63 percent.

So, in fact, whether bull or bear market, people tend to avoid buying in the broader markets on the last day of the quarter. Except, as could be expected, on the Russell 2000, where the illiquidity of the stocks that make up the index are more prone to manipulation. The results suggest a possible pairs trade going into last day of quarter: Short SMH and go long IWV, the iShares ETF for the Russell 2000.

THE END OF THE MONTH PANIC

At the end of the month, every basis point counts for fund managers. Bonuses might be dependent on the monthly result, Sharpe ratios are being calculated, track records are being dressed up and paraded to investors. If the market starts to slide mid-day then trouble is potentially brewing for the portfolio manager whose career is hanging on every tick. Consequently, if things look like they are going from bad to worse, the fund manager might irrationally sell into that panic, knowing that he can just as easily buy back his shares the next day.

Such observation suggests the following pattern:

- Buy the close when the last day of the month is down 1 percent.
- Sell at the open on the first day of the month.

Example: QQQ, 3/31/2003

The last day of March 2003, an otherwise great month for the markets, was a down day for QQQ—they closed at 25.25. The next day, when the dust cleared and portfolio managers realized they had made the mistake of a lifetime, they drove up the market pre-open so that it ended up opening at 25.44. As you can see in Figure 12.1, selling then resulted in a profit of 0.75 percent. (Also see Tables 12.1 and 12.2, page 144.)

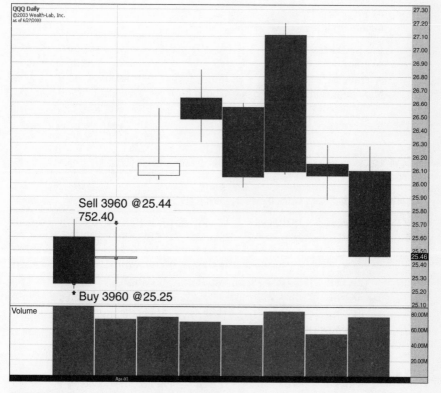

FIGURE 12.1   QQQ on March 31, 2003.

TABLE 12.1   Results for the End of Month Panic System (based on QQQ, March 4, 1999 to June 30, 2003)

	All Trades
All Trades	13
Average Profit/Loss %	1.32%
Average Bars Held	1
Winning Trades	11 (84.62%)
Average Profit %	1.66%
Average Bars Held	1
Maximum Consecutive Winning Trades	6
Losing Trades	2 (15.38%)
Average Loss %	−0.57%
Average Bars Held	1
Maximum Consecutive Losing Trades	1

TABLE 12.2   End-of-Month Panic Trades

Position	Symbol	Entry Date	Entry Price	Exit Date	Exit Price	% Change
Long	QQQ	11/30/1999	73.5	12/1/1999	74.32	1.12
Long	QQQ	12/31/1999	91.38	1/3/2000	96.19	5.26
Long	QQQ	5/31/2000	83.12	6/1/2000	85.19	2.49
Long	QQQ	9/29/2000	88.75	10/2/2000	90.25	1.69
Long	QQQ	12/29/2000	58.38	1/2/2001	58.56	0.31
Long	QQQ	1/31/2001	64.3	2/1/2001	64.55	0.39
Long	QQQ	2/28/2001	47.45	3/1/2001	46.97	−1.01
Long	QQQ	12/31/2001	38.91	1/2/2002	39.57	1.7
Long	QQQ	2/28/2002	33.78	3/1/2002	34.15	1.1
Long	QQQ	5/31/2002	30.04	6/3/2002	30	−0.13
Long	QQQ	9/30/2002	20.72	10/1/2002	20.91	0.92
Long	QQQ	11/29/2002	27.72	12/2/2002	28.42	2.53
Long	QQQ	3/31/2003	25.25	4/1/2003	25.44	0.75

In general, by the way, as Victor Niederhoffer has pointed out in *Education of a Speculator* (Wiley, 1998), developing systems for holding overnight is the best source of profits. Just as a blind example, say you bought the close of SPY every night and sold every morning. From 1993 to

2003 your average return per trade would have been 0.05 percent. Conversely, buying the open and selling the close of SPY since 1993 would have resulted in an average profit per trade of –0.01 percent (i.e., a loss of 0.01 percent per trade). Consequently, since 1993, *all* of the returns in the market have occurred overnight.

THE OUTSIDE MONTH

One more interesting month pattern is the outside month. If the market has an unusual large-range month with both the high and the low being outside the range marked off in the prior month, then that volatility has a tendency to revert to its mean in the coming month, resulting in a higher likelihood of an up month. Here is a system to take advantage of that tendency:

- Buy SPY the first day of the month when the high the prior month was higher than the high two months ago and the low the prior month was lower than the low two months ago.
- Sell on the close of the last day of the month.

Table 12.3 summarizes the results, showing an average profit of 2.20 percent per trade holding for one month. Random buying of a month is 0.78 percent. See Table 12.4 for a list of outside months since 1993.

TABLE 12.3   Outside Month, 1993–2003

	All Trades
All Trades	12
Average Profit/Loss %	2.20%
Average Bars Held	1
Winning Trades	8 (66.67%)
Average Profit %	4.31%
Average Bars Held	1
Maximum Consecutive Winning Trades	3
Losing Trades	4 (33.33%)
Average Loss %	–2.03%
Average Bars Held	1
Maximum Consecutive Losing Trades	1

TABLE 12.4 Outside Months Since 1993

Position	Symbol	Entry Date	Entry Price	Exit Date	Exit Price	% Change
Long	SPY	11/1/1994	41.9	11/1/1994	40.41	−3.56
Long	SPY	2/1/1996	58.02	2/1/1996	58.27	0.43
Long	SPY	11/3/1997	87.25	11/3/1997	89.52	2.6
Long	SPY	2/2/1998	93.88	2/2/1998	98.77	5.21
Long	SPY	7/1/1998	107.85	7/1/1998	105.7	−1.99
Long	SPY	11/2/1998	105.14	11/2/1998	110.18	4.79
Long	SPY	6/1/1999	124.17	6/1/1999	131.07	5.56
Long	SPY	11/1/1999	130.94	11/1/1999	133.61	2.04
Long	SPY	2/1/2000	134.39	2/1/2000	132.17	−1.65
Long	SPY	8/1/2000	138.8	8/1/2000	147.21	6.06
Long	SPY	10/2/2000	139.77	10/2/2000	138.49	−0.92
Long	SPY	4/1/2003	85.25	4/1/2003	91.91	7.81

Ten Percent Down— Panic 101

S entiment indicators have been useful timing tools in the 2000–2002 bear market and have flown in the face of the commonly used adage, "The trend is your friend." The question is: Is it possible to develop a trading system that takes advantage of these extremes in despair? Let us look at two different systems, one for stocks and the other for indexes, where the panic levels are extreme. We will try to find out what happens if we blindly take the other side of the panic.

THE 10 PERCENT PULLBACK

The idea is simple: Buy a stock that is 10 percent lower than the prior day's close. But what could happen to cause such a drop? Any number of things:

- Massive earnings warning.
- SEC investigation announced.
- The company fails several FDA trials.
- The CEO skips the country and all the money is missing from the bank account.
- Etc.

Well, OK, that makes sense then. I mean, if the company goes from $2 a share in profits to $2 a share in losses, then maybe it deserves to fall 10 percent during the course of a day. Who would want to own it? Certainly not the mutual funds who might be dumping tens of millions of shares that day. Definitely not the brokers who put their clients into the stock and now they are thoroughly embarrassed at the result. And feeding on top of this are the trend-following day traders who are shorting the trend. A stock in this situation becomes a death spiral.

So here is a system for taking advantage of a market panic:

- Buy a stock that is 10 percent lower than the prior day's close.
- Sell at the end of the day.

Consider all S&P Mid-Cap 400 stocks over the past five years. I chose mid-cap to avoid any so-called size effect, but the same test can obviously be performed on any subset of stocks.

Assume we start off with $1M and use $50K (5 percent of portfolio) per trade. See the results listed in Table 13.1 (see page 151). Since January 1, 1997, the system permitted about 8,200 trades and 60 percent of the trades were profitable, with an average profit per trade of 1.4 percent. The maximum drawdown of the system was –3.5 percent, as opposed to –40 percent for a buy and hold strategy (as evidenced by the thick wavy line in the equity curve in Figure 13.1).

In a variation of that system:

- Buy a stock that is 10 percent lower than the prior day's close.
- Sell after holding for one month.

As a test, consider all Nasdaq 100 stocks since 1995. Assume starting with $1M and using $2,000 (0.2 percent of equity) per trade. See the annual returns shown in Figure 13.2 (see page 150) and listed in Table 13.2 (see page 152). The results can be summarized as follows:

Average annual return: 13.89 percent

Standard deviation of returns: 9.07

Sharpe ratio: 1.53

Average return per trade: 8.16 percent

Average return per winning trade: 28.82 percent

Average return per losing trade: –18.67 percent

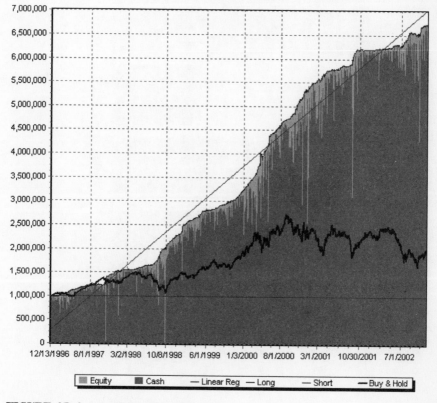

FIGURE 13.1   Portfolio equity curve.

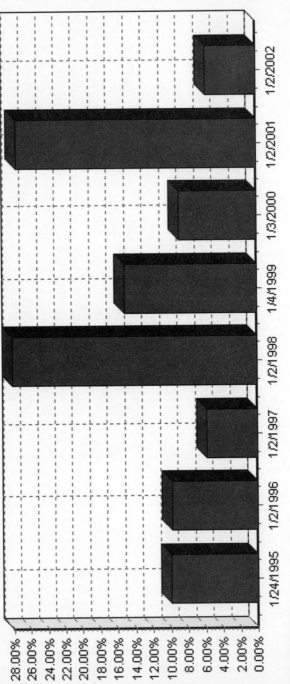

FIGURE 13.2 Annual returns.

TABLE 13.1 Ten Percent Pullback System

	All Trades	Buy & Hold
Starting Capital	$1,000,000.00	$1,000,000.00
Ending Capital	$6,744,820.50	$1,998,198.00
Net Profit	$5,744,820.50	$998,198.00
Net Profit %	574.48%	99.82%
Exposure %	7.50%	100%
Risk-Adjusted Return	7,663.94%	99.82%
All Trades	8,197	397
Average Profit/Loss	$700.84	$2,514.35
Average Profit/Loss %	1.42%	99.85%
Average Bars Held	1.00	1,499.00
Winning Trades	4968 (60.61%)	282 (71.03%)
Gross Profit	$12,969,821.00	$1,101,028.75
Average Profit	$2,610.67	$3,904.36
Average Profit %	5.30%	155.07%
Average Bars Held	1.00	1,499.00
Maximum Consecutive Winning Trades	41	14
Losing Trades	3229 (39.39%)	115 (28.97%)
Gross Loss	$−7,224,984.00	$−102,831.17
Average Loss	$−2,237.53	$−894.18
Average Loss %	−4.54%	−35.56%
Average Bars Held	1.00	1,499.00
Maximum Consecutive Losing Trades	25	5
Maximum Drawdown	−3.54%	−40.43%
Maximum Drawdown $	$−142,059.75	$−1,107,053.25
Maximum Drawdown Date	4/14/2000	10/9/2002
Standard Error	$335,618.53	$258,692.67
Risk Reward Ratio	3.35	0.91
Sharpe Ratio of Trades	3.24	0.16

EXTREME ADVANCES-DECLINES

Sometimes the extremity of a panic should not be measured just by depth (for instance, a 10 percent selloff), but by breadth (for instance, every stock in the universe went down today). While it is unlikely that every single stock goes down even in a crash (in fact, gold stocks usually go up then), it does seem like an extreme if for every one stock that is up, seven stocks are down. For the S&P Mid-Cap 400, a ratio of 7 down stocks for 1 up stock would translate to the number of advancing stocks minus the number of declining stocks being lower than −300 (50 stocks up, 350 stocks down).

TABLE 13.2 Annual Returns

Period Starting	$ Return	% Return	% Maximum DD	Exposure	Entries	Exits
1/24/1995	99,167.25	9.92	−1.48	5.76	351	301
1/2/1996	108,217.50	9.85	−2.86	8.24	569	598
1/2/1997	70,164.13	5.81	−2.12	8.25	637	605
1/2/1998	358,756.75	28.08	−5.51	12.44	989	986
1/4/1999	247,274.00	15.11	−2.01	8.91	921	919
1/3/2000	168,689.00	8.96	−14.45	23.24	3,112	2,799
1/2/2001	565,377.88	27.55	−16.89	18.73	2,475	2,770
1/2/2002	153,366.75	5.86	−7.50	12.49	1,867	1,764

The system I propose for taking advantage of this measure of the extremity of market panic is:

- Buy the Mid-Cap ($MDY) index at the close of the market if the number of advancing stocks minus the number of declining stocks is lower than −300.
- Sell in two months.

Since 1996, the system makes the trades shown in Table 13.3. You can see that not a lot of trades would have been generated—only nine, six of which are profitable. However it is interesting to see that those days of extreme market reactions to the downside, where everyone was selling everything, called significant market bottoms over that time period.

TABLE 13.3 Trades

Entry Date	Entry Price	Exit Date	Exit Price	% Change	Bars Held
10/27/1997	308.70	12/24/1997	319.28	3.41	41
8/27/1998	305.25	10/26/1998	322.30	5.56	41
4/14/2000	431.37	6/14/2000	489.55	13.47	41
3/12/2001	478.61	5/9/2001	510.71	6.69	41
6/14/2001	509.98	8/13/2001	501.93	−1.60	41
9/17/2001	445.19	11/13/2001	479.45	7.67	41
6/3/2002	515.82	7/31/2002	441.27	−14.47	41
8/2/2002	419.70	10/3/2002	399.18	−4.91	41
10/4/2002	389.47	Open	Open	15.18	40

CONCLUSION

Buying panic is difficult. During those moments of panic it is not likely that I can pick up my calculator and coolly figure out how much money I am about to make. More likely, I am thinking, "It's the end of the world!" and planning out my log cabin in Canada. Nevertheless, it is at these moments where opportunity gives birth.

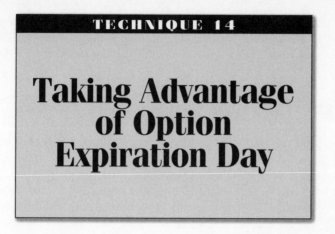

Taking Advantage of Option Expiration Day

To identify a trading edge one must first pray to the gods of efficient market theory (EMT) that they turn the other way for a short while. Rational, efficient markets, with all information baked in, do not make for exploitable edges. However, if there is any day in a month where it can be claimed that the EMT gods take a short vacation, it has to be the third Friday of each month—option expiration day (OED).

Everybody has a theory as to what happens on option expiration day. Some that I have read about only in the past week (as I write this it is the day after a "quadruple witching day") include:

- Stocks gravitate towards round numbers.
- Extreme countertrend moves occur in the last hour.
- The market tends to trend the week before option expiration day.
- Fade the market at the end of option expiration day.

And on and on. Everyone wants to game the market that day, and probably more money is lost by traders on that day then any other day of the month.

Let us look at a couple of ideas that have withstood the test of time and have demonstrated results that are statistically significant when placed around option expiration day. None of these ideas by themselves generate an enormous number of trades (there are only so many option expiration days and we are still looking for extreme conditions), but taken as a group they add up.

All data used for testing the following systems are from the S&P and the NDX in the years 1988–2003. The trading vehicle could be SPY or S&P futures, or QQQ or NDX futures depending on the index we are looking at.

OED SYSTEM #1: DON'T FIGHT THE TREND

In general it is not that great an idea to buy a four-month high. Four-month closing highs have occurred on the S&P 407 times since 1988. Buying on those days and closing out the position one week later has resulted in a successful trade in 58 percent of the occurrences (239 trades) with an expected value of 0.17 percent per trade, counting both winners and losers. Basically, the results are slightly less than expected given that the average daily return on the S&P 500 is about 0.04 percent.

However, when the following three conditions occur it becomes profitable to buy:

1. The S&P 500 makes a 4-month (80 trading days) closing high.
2. The VIX closes within 20 percent of its 4-month low.
3. It is the Friday the week before option expiration week (one week before option expiration day).

If these conditions occur, then buy on the close of that Friday. Then sell on the close of option expiration day one week later.

The results are shown in Table 14.1 and Table 14.2. In summary, there is an average gain of 1.14 percent per trade. Taking out the VIX condition still results in a decent system but one not as strong: 17 out of 23 successful trades with an average gain of 0.65 percent per trade. Leaving in the VIX condition but taking out the condition that states OED occurs in one week leaves us with 191 out of 304 successful trades and an average gain of 0.28 percent. It appears that the proximity of OED is critical to the trade.

For example, as shown in Figure 14.1 (see page 158), the S&P 500 hit a four-month closing high at 1396.06, the VIX had a four-month closing low at 19.63, and OED was one week away. Buying at the close and holding for that week resulted in a 1.86 percent gain.

TABLE 14.1 OED System #1—Results

	All Trades	Long Trades
All Trades	17	17
Average Profit/Loss %	1.14%	1.14%
Average Bars Held	5	5
Winning Trades	15 (88.24%)	15 (88.24%)
Average Profit %	1.38%	1.38%
Average Bars Held	5	5
Maximum Consecutive Winning Trades	9	9
Losing Trades	2 (11.76%)	2 (11.76%)
Average Loss %	−0.68%	−0.68%
Average Bars Held	5	5
Maximum Consecutive Losing Trades	2	2

TABLE 14.2 OED System #1—The Trades

Entry Date	Entry Price	Exit Date	Exit Price	% Change	MAE %	MFE %
1/13/1989	283.87	1/20/1989	286.63	0.97	−0.43	1.42
4/14/1989	301.36	4/21/1989	309.61	2.74	−0.22	2.74
5/12/1989	313.84	5/19/1989	321.24	2.36	0	2.4
7/14/1989	331.84	7/21/1989	335.9	1.22	−0.33	1.68
5/11/1990	352	5/18/1990	354.64	0.75	−0.01	1.82
2/8/1991	359.35	2/15/1991	369.06	2.7	−0.01	3.11
4/12/1991	380.4	4/19/1991	384.2	1	−0.43	2.85
2/10/1995	481.46	2/17/1995	481.97	0.11	−0.12	0.85
3/10/1995	489.57	3/17/1995	495.52	1.22	−0.04	1.45
4/13/1995	509.23	4/21/1995	508.49	−0.15	−1.58	0.55
5/12/1995	525.55	5/19/1995	519.19	−1.21	−1.61	0.67
9/8/1995	572.68	9/15/1995	583.35	1.86	0	2.16
9/13/1996	680.54	9/20/1996	687.03	0.95	−0.22	0.96
11/8/1996	730.82	11/15/1996	737.62	0.93	−0.38	1.52
2/12/1998	1,024.14	2/20/1998	1,034.21	0.98	−0.63	0.98
7/9/1999	1,403.28	7/16/1999	1,418.78	1.1	−1.2	1.1
11/12/1999	1,396.06	11/19/1999	1,422.00	1.86	−0.27	2.1

FIGURE 14.1　S&P on November 12, 1999.

OED SYSTEM #2: DON'T FIGHT THE TREND, PART II

If the day before option expiration day the market is up 1.5 percent (on the S&P 500), then buy the close and sell the close the next day. Table 14.3 and Table 14.4 show the results.

TABLE 14.3 The Results

	All Trades
All Trades	12
Average Profit/Loss %	0.70%
Average Bars Held	1
Winning Trades	12 (100.00%)
Average Profit %	0.70%
Average Bars Held	1
Maximum Consecutive Winning Trades	12
Losing Trades	0 (0.00%)
Average Loss %	0.00%
Average Bars Held	0
Maximum Consecutive Losing Trades	0

TABLE 14.4 The Trades

Entry Date	Entry Price	Exit Date	Exit Price	% Change
10/20/1988	282.88	10/21/1988	283.66	0.28
10/19/1989	347.13	10/20/1989	347.16	0.01
10/18/1990	305.74	10/19/1990	312.48	2.2
1/17/1991	327.97	1/18/1991	332.23	1.3
12/19/1996	745.76	12/20/1996	748.87	0.42
11/20/1997	958.98	11/21/1997	963.09	0.43
10/15/1998	1,047.49	10/16/1998	1,056.42	0.85
12/17/1998	1,179.98	12/18/1998	1,188.03	0.68
3/16/2000	1,458.47	3/17/2000	1,464.47	0.41
10/19/2000	1,388.76	10/20/2000	1,396.93	0.59
10/17/2002	879.2	10/18/2002	884.39	0.59
11/14/2002	904.27	11/15/2002	909.83	0.61

OED SYSTEM #3: SHORT THE NASDAQ

First of all, it should be noted that the Nasdaq 100 and OED are not friends. In general, shorting the Nasdaq 100 (through QQQ or NDX futures) on the close before OED and covering at the close of OED has had the results shown in Table 14.5. These results are significantly different from the average result of –0.07 percent, if one were to short the NDX on a random day.

The results get better the more ^NDX is down the day before OED (see Table 14.6). Even better, if the QQQs, on OED, gap up higher than the close the day before, one can short with impunity and close out at the end of the day (see Table 14.7 and Table 14.8).

TABLE 14.5   OED System #3—Results

	All Trades
All Trades	176
Average Profit/Loss %	0.42%
Average Bars Held	1
Winning Trades	99 (56.25%)
Average Profit %	1.44%
Average Bars Held	1
Maximum Consecutive Winning Trades	7
Losing Trades	77 (43.75%)
Average Loss %	–0.89%
Average Bars Held	1
Maximum Consecutive Losing Trades	4

TABLE 14.6   The Results

NDX Down More Than	Result	Average Return
1%	25 out of 38	0.99%
1.50%	18 out of 29	1.06%
2%	13 out of 18	1.48%
3%	8 out of 11	1.70%

TABLE 14.7 OED System #3 With Gap Up

	All Trades
All Trades	17
Average Profit/Loss %	0.72%
Average Bars Held	1
Winning Trades	14 (82.35%)
Average Profit %	1.09%
Average Bars Held	1
Maximum Consecutive Winning Trades	8
Losing Trades	3 (17.65%)
Average Loss %	−1.05%
Average Bars Held	1
Maximum Consecutive Losing Trades	2

TABLE 14.8 OED System #3 With Gap Up—Trades

Entry Date	Entry Price	Exit Date	Exit Price	% Change
9/17/1999	62.03	9/17/1999	63.31	−2.06
12/17/1999	84.5	12/17/1999	83.78	0.85
1/21/2000	96.5	1/21/2000	96.25	0.26
2/18/2000	102.62	2/18/2000	98.44	4.07
6/16/2000	94.75	6/16/2000	94.25	0.53
8/18/2000	95.94	8/18/2000	95.25	0.72
9/15/2000	93.12	9/15/2000	91.31	1.94
11/17/2000	73.19	11/17/2000	72.83	0.49
1/19/2001	68.14	1/19/2001	66.31	2.69
12/21/2001	39.42	12/21/2001	39.48	−0.15
3/15/2002	36.89	3/15/2002	37.23	−0.92
4/19/2002	35.05	4/19/2002	34.46	1.68
5/17/2002	33.29	5/17/2002	32.93	1.08
9/20/2002	21.83	9/20/2002	21.67	0.73
12/20/2002	25.33	12/20/2002	25.32	0.04
3/21/2003	27.21	3/21/2003	27.17	0.15
4/21/2003	26.94	4/21/2003	26.92	0.07

CONCLUSION

Throughout the history of the markets there is a ubiquitous character, somewhat shady, called "They." Every now and then I hear: "They" are taking it up today. "They" are going to push it down. "They" are going to screw the most people they can. Most of the time this master manipulator fades into the background and lets the markets do what they will. But if there is ever a day where "They" makes a grand appearance, it is option expiration day. By testing and asking the right questions one can make the most of this appearance.

TECHNIQUE 15

Extreme Convertible Arbitrage

In the X Games, what makes extreme sports such as snowboarding, bike stunts, skateboarding, and the like so fascinating is that the risks often seem much greater than normal sports such as baseball or football. The reality is that more athletes are injured in those more mainstream sports, but the thrill of the X Games keeps people coming back for more each year. In extreme convertible arbitrage we see that the public basically thinks a company is going bankrupt and hence prices the preferred stocks of those companies to give exorbitant yields. These extreme yields keep us on the edge of our seats, and, hopefully, the rewards are great.

Convertible arbitrage consists of the simultaneous buying of a long convertible security and shorting of the underlying common stock. The idea is to hedge the long position with the short so that any changes in price are neutralized. Meanwhile, one can collect the yield and ideally benefit further if the convertible is in the money, that is, the stock is trading higher than the conversion price, in which case the convertible should rise faster than the stock.

There are many esoteric ways to value a convertible security, none of which we concern ourselves with in this technique. The system described here plays a mean reversion strategy combined with traditional convertible arbitrage. We buy a pair after the underlying stock does down significantly in a single day. The reasons it might go down are varied—perhaps an SEC investigation, perhaps an asbestos lawsuit, perhaps an earnings warning. In many cases, the convertible bond will irrationally follow the stock down, resulting in a yield up to 2,000 basis points higher than the 10-year Treasury note.

Funds specializing in convertible arbitrage usually have relationships with the various bond desks on Wall Street. When a company issues a convertible, the bond desks call the funds and say "company XYZ is issuing convertible ABC yielding 5 percent and converting at 50 in 2007." The funds make a decision to buy or sell, and when they buy, they hedge part of their position by shorting the underlying common, hence locking in the 5 percent yield and participating in upside if the stock moves higher than the convert price. If the company falters in its plan and spirals into bankruptcy, then this is often the best situation as the convertible is almost certainly senior to the common stock. So when the common goes to 0, the convertible will still have some value left and the fund has probably made more money on the short side than the long side (of course, "men make plans and God laughs").

However, this scenario is too complicated for our purposes. Many convertible securities (and other bondlike instruments) trade on the main exchanges as preferred stocks. Focusing on just preferred stock arbitrage has many advantages:

- One does not have to call bond desks to get obscure prices on illiquid bonds. Using any broker or electronic trading platform, one can trade preferred stocks.
- Unlike bonds, the prices of preferred stocks are often correlated to the common stock. As we will see, this correlation is often irrational and can lead to successful mean reversion strategies on preferred stocks.
- There is less interest rate risk. The universe of preferred stock holders (including mutual funds, 401(k)s, etc.) intersects more broadly with the universe of common equity holders. This intersection combined with an increased correlation to the underlying equity leaves preferred stocks less susceptible to price changes in response to large changes in interest rates. With interest rates, as of this writing, at 45-year lows, anything we can do to avoid interest rate risk is helpful at this point.
- Flight to quality is less of a concern. Convertible arbitrage in 1994 and 1998 was affected by a flight out of riskier bonds and into blue chip so-called safe stocks. While partially shielded by the hedges on the shorts, convert arbitrage strategies faltered in these years. Again, since there is a large overlap between preferred holders and common equity holders, we are less affected by these redemptions.

PREFERRED ARBITRAGE SYSTEM

- Identify preferred stocks where the preferred and the common have both fallen 10 percent on a single day. Only play pairs where the preferred is now yielding greater than 8 percent.
- At close, buy the preferred and short the common by a factor of 2:1 dollar ratio. The ratio leans toward the bullish side (even taking into account the fact that preferreds move slower than the common) to take advantage of mean reversion tendencies in both the common and the preferred, but hedges the risk against a free fall. Typically a 2:1 ratio might not be good enough because preferreds sometimes move *much* slower than the underlying common. However, the fact that both the preferred and the common have fallen 10 percent in one day demonstrates that they are, at least temporarily, moving in sync.
- Sell at the sooner of a 10 percent profit on the pair or one dividend payment, or if you decide to hold longer to maximize the benefits of the higher dividend yield, then after one quarter seek to neutralize the risk by adjusting the hedging ratio as follows:

$$\frac{\% \text{ Change in Common Stock over Prior Month}}{\% \text{ Change in Preferred over Prior Month}}$$

So if the common is moving three times as fast as the preferred, the new ratio should be 3:1. If the common is moving half as fast, then the new ratio should be 1:2.

Do preferred stocks tend to mean revert? When plugging in a list of 150 preferreds into the pullback system described in Technique 3, the result of buying a 10 percent pullback in one day and holding for one month is 13.33 percent average profit per trade with a standard deviation of 35 percent. The standard deviation alone is enough to make me want to hedge. Although the 13 percent per trade is nice, a string of below average returns could cause some pain. Hedging the volatility while locking in the yield is the goal.

THE RISKS

Before analyzing an example, it is important to understand further all the risks in the trade.

- Bankruptcy of the company can occur. This risk is hedged by the use of the short position as well as various option strategies that can be applied. In a bankruptcy the preferred often does not fall as far as the common. Depending on the type of security, there is also protection via assets as well as insurance guaranties.
- The dividend is deferred. It is important to understand that the dividend cannot be cancelled but only deferred; interest is also earned on the deferred portion. The short position offers protection in the case of a price decrease (in most cases, the common has decreased faster in value on a deferral which might imply bankruptcy).
- The spread is not aligned. Unfortunately hedging is more often art than science. The 2:1 ratio mentioned previously is a best guess in general. However, if this ratio does not appear to be working, then adjust according to the recent percentage price change of the common over the recent percentage change in the preferred.
- Interest rate risk exists. Because of the drop in price of the preferred, the preferred security has more characteristics of an equity than a bond in terms of the way it trades. The yield is so much higher than standard interest rates that it would require a much greater than normal move to dissuade investors from pursuing the higher yield.

EXAMPLE: SEE/SEE-A

On July 29, 2002, shares of Sealed Air closed at 37.77. The maker of bubble wrap was enjoying consistently improving cash flows and the stock was acting accordingly. Nevertheless, the next morning it was announced that an asbestos case that was affecting WR Grace was potentially going to have ramifications on Sealed Air because of the acquisition of Cryovac from Grace. The question at hand was, did Grace avoid paying off the asbestos responsibilities of Cryovac by spinning it out to SEE and then going into bankruptcy? In the agreement with Sealed Air, Grace assumed all responsibility for any debts incurred from the asbestos claims on Cryovac, but it is unclear what this meant once Grace went into Chapter 11. A judge ruled that Sealed Air might be responsible, and the shares crashed the next day, opening at 19.80 and going as low as 13.29 before closing at 14.51 on triple the average daily volume (see Figure 15.1).

Many people were playing the dip-buying strategy of buying SEE, and this strategy would have paid off handsomely since the next day the shares closed over 20 percent higher at 17.25. However, the more interesting play would have been to buy shares of the preferred, SEE-A and short the common. SEE-A fell from a close to 39.50 on July 29 to a close of 25.25 the next

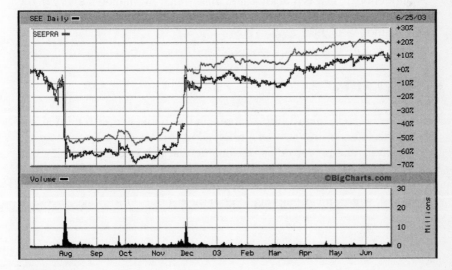

FIGURE 15.1 SEE/SEE-A.

day, and to 18.05 the day after that. At that level, the preferred stock was paying a dividend of 11 percent.

On the one hand, if SEE's problems were sufficient to send it into bankruptcy, then the shares of Sealed Air common stock would have suffered much more than the preferred as the common comes below the preferred in the capital structure of the company. In other words, if the company had any chance at all of emerging from bankruptcy, the preferred shareholders would get paid before the common shareholders. On the other hand, if the company was going to emerge unscathed, then the purchasers of the SEE preferred would get the benefit of purchasing an 11 percent yielding instrument that also had the potential of going up quickly in face value.

Sure enough, it was quickly ruled that Sealed Air had no liability in the asbestos case. As of this writing, shares of SEE preferred are at 51.06 and SEE common is 46.99.

CONCLUSION

As we have seen in many of the systems in this book, people tend to panic first, think later. In the case of preferred arbitrage, the yields get so far from what can be perceived as reasonable that it is worth examining and seeing if we can benefit. Since the common and the preferred are often closely correlated in these cases, it is possible to largely nullify the bankruptcy risk while still attempting to grab the benefits of the huge yields.

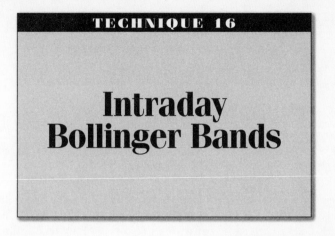

Intraday Bollinger Bands

There is a good reason why most day traders go broke. The market does not really like to give up too much money in very short periods of time. Most of the systems described in this book are for one or more days. Even these systems make the mistress of the markets anxious and require constant overseeing and testing to confirm that they still hold true. To shorten the length of time from days to minutes is perhaps testing the wrath of the markets too much. Nevertheless, there are moments when the fears and petty greeds of the market participants are too much and opportunity is allowed to strike.

Even if one uses a purely systematic approach, day trading and trading in general is not for the faint of heart. Drawdowns are a fact of life, losing trades are a fact of life, stresses beyond any normal day job become commonplace. I have never been described as a particularly athletic person, but every morning I wake up early (between 4:00 AM and 5:00 AM), take a several mile walk, read a couple of the morning papers, and then by 7 AM I am ready to start plugging in my systems to see if the futures markets or the equities pre-markets are giving me any signals. By 8 AM I usually have my morning plan all ready and have outlined what I am going to do for as many contingencies as possible. Without thorough preparation and a healthy body and mind there is essentially zero chance of success in this game.

In Technique 5 we looked at what happens when one buys a stock if it goes lower than the 10-day Bollinger band using 1.5 standard deviations. In this technique, rather than looking at daily bars, we look at 5-minute bars and ask the question: What happens when a stock goes decisively through its 10-period Bollinger band using 2 standard deviations?

FIVE-MINUTE BOLLINGER BAND SYSTEM

On a chart of 5-minute bars for a stock, plot out the 10-bar moving average and the Bollinger bands for 2 standard deviations on either side of the average. Then apply the following system:

- Buy when the stock falls 3 percent below its lower band. Hold until at least the end of the 5-minute bar where the stock was bought.
- Sell when the stock hits a 1 percent profit target *or* at the end of the second bar after the stock was bought.

The critical issue is how to keep track of all the stocks one is interested in. Before the open, use charting software such as eSignal or TradeStation, or Wealth-Lab (which is the software I use for all of my testing) to identify the Bollinger band levels for each stock. It is then possible with all of these packages to set up alerts and even interface with direct-access brokers, such as Interactive Brokers or Cybertrader, to actually make the trades automatically.

EXAMPLES

The key in all of these examples is time. Basically, the market has such an extreme and quick selloff in order to trigger this system that the stock either bounces back immediately or flounders about. If the latter, then we promptly get out since we are only looking for our profit target within the ten minutes following the entry bar.

ORCL, 5/20/2002, 10:30 AM

Merrill Lynch, in a post-Blodget fury of tech pessimism, reiterated a broad-sweeping recommendation the morning of May 20, 2002, to sell technology stocks into any strength. While their prediction proved mildly prophetic for all of two months, anybody short technology at May 2002 levels would have been killed over the following year. Nevertheless, the panic to get out of the popular tech issues, for instance ORCL, was enough to trigger a signal on ORCL at 10:30 AM at 8.73 (Figure 16.1). In a brief flurry of selling, it hit 3 percent below its lower band, which it had been steadily walking down all morning. Buying at the critical level and holding until the open of the next 5-minute bar would have resulted in a quick 3.3 percent profit with the sale at 9.02.

Sell 11451
@9.02
3,300.20

Buy 11451
@8.73

ORCL 5 Minute
©2003 Wealth-Lab, Inc.
as of 7/2/2003

Volume

FIGURE 16.1 ORCL on May 20, 2002.

MSFT, 4/3/2000

Many of examples occur close to the open of the day, which is the time when there is the most volatility and also the most panic. The market has had all night to hear and absorb news, and thus the open is when the most participants at once are acting on that news.

Look at Figure 16.2. On April 3, 2000, MSFT gapped down and triggered signals for two five-minute bars in a row, at 9:30 AM at the open and 5 minutes later at 9:40 AM. The first signal was sold off at the close of the second bar at 47.69 for a 1 percent profit, and the second signal, which was bought at the open of the second bar at 47.44, was promptly sold at 47.91 for a 1 percent profit.

AMAT, 11/12/01

On the morning of November 12, 2001, a plane crashed near Kennedy airport. The crash was not apparently an act of terrorism but nobody knew that at the time. Futures spiked lower and the tech stocks, which were hit hardest during the week after September 11, 2001, suffered a minicrash immediately prior to the open. Being alert and capitalizing on the panic would have enabled one to buy AMAT, which triggered a buy signal at its premarket low at 18.20 when it hit 3 percent lower than its lower Bollinger band (Figure 16.3, page 174). Holding to the close of that 5-minute bar would have enabled one to sell immediately at 19.33 for a 6.15 percent profit.

PROFITING FROM PANIC

What if on any of these occasions when there is a selling panic, the panic is justified? There are essentially two answers:

1. Almost every time in the past century when there has been a selling panic, it has been unjustified.
2. Even the justified selling panics often are still worth buying.

Take a look at what happened to the Dow after the following events thought to be world-class disasters at the times of their occurrences:

- John F. Kennedy's assassination, November 22, 1963—Day 1: –3 percent; one month later: +7.6 percent.
- Start of Korean War, June 26, 1950—Day 1: –4.6 percent; two months later: –3 percent.

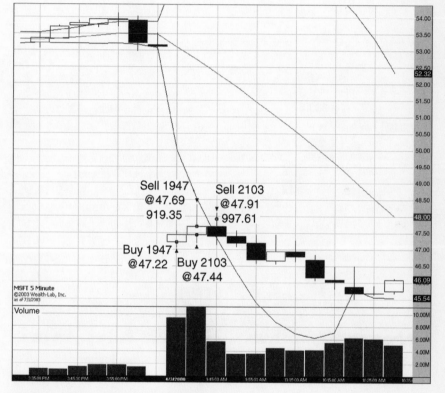

FIGURE 16.2   MSFT on April 3, 2000.

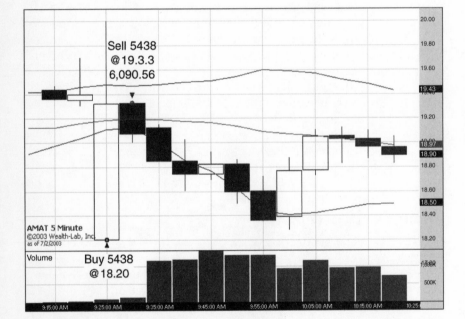

Sell 5438
@19.3.3
6,090.56

AMAT 5 Minute
©2003 Wealth-Lab, Inc
as of 7/2/2003

Volume   **Buy 5438**
                  @18.20

FIGURE 16.3   AMAT on November 12, 2001.

- Gerald Ford pardoned Richard Nixon (not as horrible as terrorism, obviously, but symptomatic of the complete distrust America had for its leaders)—Day 1: –2.7 percent; two months later: +7.4 percent.
- Pearl Harbor, December 7, 1941—Day 1: –4.2 percent; two months later: –5 percent (the market did not go higher than Pearl Harbor day until October 8, 1942).
- Cuban missile crisis, October 26, 1962—Day 1: –1.9 percent; two months later: +12 percent.
- Destruction of the Twin Towers in New York City by terrorists, September 11, 2001—Day 1: –5.2 percent; two months later: +4 percent.

In every case when it seemed like the world was falling apart it paid to be a buyer of U.S. equities. Will this pattern continue forever into the future? We don't know. However, buying panic has *always* to this point been a reliable method of making money in the markets and this pattern seems likely to continue for some time. Another thing to note is that panic will never go away—there will always be the latest negative employment report, murmurings of war, an earnings rumor, a merger and acquisitions deal that got squashed, and so on that will drive people into another selling frenzy. Frenzies are irrational and must be bought. If you are worried that "this time things are different," then keep your position sizes small (which should be done for all of these systems anyway).

RESULTS OF THE 5-MINUTE BOLLINGER BAND SYSTEM

(Feb 2, 2002–June 30, 2003) See Table 16.1 for results of the 5-minute Bollinger band system applied to the following basket of stocks: AMAT, BRCM, CSCO, DELL, INTC, JDSU, MSFT, ORCL, QQQ, SEBL, and SUNW, for February 2, 2002 to June 30, 2003. These are the highest volume Nasdaq 100 stocks. You can see that the average return is 2.77 percent per trade across 113 trades with 92 percent success.

It is also worth examining the results of this system per stock to which we are applying this system. For instance, the results on MSFT from 1999 to June 30, 2003, are shown in Table 16.2 and on ORCL in Table 16.3 (see page 177).

Raising the barrier so that we are looking for a stock to penetrate 2 percent lower than its 10,2 Bollinger band (10-day moving average, 2 standard deviations) gives the result shown in Table 16.4 (see page 177) for ORCL. We can see that in this case the system increases the number of trades but lowers the average profit per trade.

TABLE 16.1 5 Min BB System, 2/2/02–6/30/03

	All Trades
All Trades	113
Average Profit/Loss %	2.77%
Average Bars Held	1.46
Winning Trades	104 (92.04%)
Average Profit %	3.22%
Average Bars Held	1.12
Maximum Consecutive Winning Tables	30
Losing Trades	9 (7.96%)
Average Loss %	−2.43%
Average Bars Held	5.44
Maximum Consecutive Losing Trades	2

TABLE 16.2 5 Min BB (Just MSFT)

	All Trades
All Trades	17
Average Profit/Loss %	1.99%
Average Bars Held	1.71
Winning Trades	14 (82.35%)
Average Profit %	2.63%
Average Bars Held	1
Maximum Consecutive Winning Tables	10
Losing Trades	3 (17.65%)
Average Loss %	−0.99%
Average Bars Held	5
Maximum Consecutive Losing Tables	2

TABLE 16.3 5 Min BB—ORCL

	All Trades
All Trades	49
Average Profit/Loss %	2.12%
Average Bars Held	1.59
Winning Trades	46 (93.88%)
Gross Profit	$106,970.12
Average Profit %	2.34%
Average Bars Held	1.37
Maximum Consecutive Winning Trades	34
Losing Trades	3 (6.12%)
Average Loss %	−1.20%
Average Bars Held	5
Maximum Consecutive Losing Trades	1

TABLE 16.4 5 Min BB Variation—ORCL

	All Trades
All Trades	176
Average Profit/Loss %	1.12%
Average Bars Held	1.91
Winning Trades	155 (88.07%)
Average Profit %	1.52%
Average Bars Held	1.5
Maximum Consecutive Winning Trades	26
Losing Trades	21 (11.93%)
Average Loss %	−1.84%
Average Bars Held	5
Maximum Consecutive Losing Trades	2

CONCLUSION

Every day in the market is actually extraordinarily volatile. The average 7 percent return in the markets since 1950 does not really express the volatility of the journey. Every day is often up or down 2 percent, not just once but several times. To be able to get pieces of those 2 percent moves and have those pieces add up is the mark of a successful trader. Gut feeling will not do it in the long run, but thoroughly researched systems such as the one described in this technique will.

All Good Things Come in Fours ("4" Is a Magic Number)

I am always very impressed with the people who draw upon chaos theory, quantum mechanics, digital signal processing, and other esoteric far-flung sciences in order to develop indicators to trade the markets. If you are a chaos theoretician and have five degrees and various awards and then develop a "chaotic indicator" to trade the markets, who isn't going to invest in your hedge fund? That said, I have yet to see one of those indicators actually work and more often than not there is more of a marketing element in these ideas than an actual trading idea.

Sometimes simple is best, although even the simplest idea needs to be thoroughly tested before being exploited. For instance, many people like to buy the market after four down days, and short the market after four up days. Both ideas make intuitive sense. In one case, it is pretty clear the market is not going to zero, so how many down days in a row can we actually have? Similarly, markets cannot go straight up forever or we would be at Dow 30,000 already. So it is reasonable after four up days that we should be able to short the market.

That said, after four down days, many die-hard longs give up hope and get ready to pack it in for the new bear market. Let us see what the truth is.

FOUR DOWN DAYS

- Buy the close of the SPY (ETF for the S&P) on the fourth consecutive down close.
- Sell one day later.

Example: SPY, 5/25/99 and 6/11/99

Consider SPY in the spring of 1999 (Figure 17.1). In late May the Consumer Price Index data came out and showed a spike in inflation. It became pretty clear that the interest-rate party was over. Federal Reserve Chairman Alan Greenspan had kept things going after the Long Term Capital Management disaster in 1998, but now there was a serious threat of inflation and interest rates were going to have to rise. For the next year and a half Greenspan set steady increases until January 3, 2001.

Meanwhile, once the market realized that rates were going to rise, the market started to slide. First on May 25 we had the fourth consecutive down close in a row. Buying on the close and selling the next day resulted in a 1.11 percent profit. Then two and a half weeks later, on June 11, 1999, we had four down days in a row again and a buy signal was triggered for SPY at 123.86, which sold at the close one day later at 123.99 for only a 0.10 percent profit.

The results are shown in Table 17.1, listing a 73 percent accuracy rate with an average profit per trade of 0.66 percent.

TABLE 17.1   4 Down Days and Buy—1993–6/03

	All Trades
All Trades	80
Average Profit/Loss %	0.66%
Average Bars Held	1
Winning Trades	59 (73.75%)
Average Profit %	1.33%
Average Bars Held	1
Maximum Consecutive Winning Trades	15
Losing Trades	21 (26.25%)
Average Loss %	−1.23%
Average Bars Held	1
Maximum Consecutive Losing Trades	2

Example: QQQ, 4/24/99 to 6/30/03

The same system but with QQQ from March 24, 1999 to June 30, 2003 has the result shown in Table 17.2 (see page 182), listing a 66 percent accuracy with an average profit per trade of 0.94 percent.

So now the question is: Does this system work in reverse? The answer is: not really.

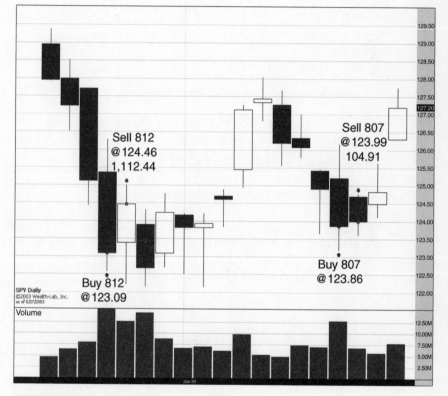

FIGURE 17.1   SPY, May and June 1999.

TABLE 17.2   4 Down Days and Buy—QQQ

	All Trades
All Trades	42
Average Profit/Loss %	0.94%
Average Bars Held	1
Winning Trades	28 (66.67%)
Average Profit %	3.14%
Average Bars Held	1
Maximum Consecutive Winning Trades	6
Losing Trades	14 (33.33%)
Average Loss %	–3.46%
Average Bars Held	1
Maximum Consecutive Losing Trades	1

FOUR UP DAYS AND SHORT (NOT A RECOMMENDED SYSTEM)

- Short on the close of the fourth consecutive up close.
- Cover one day later.

The results of applying this system to SPY from 1993 to June 30, 2003, are shown in Table 17.3. There we can see a 0.06 percent average profit per trade and only a 52 percent success rate. After commissions and slippage,

TABLE 17.3   4 Up Days and Short

	All Trades
All Trades	148
Average Profit/Loss %	0.06%
Average Bars Held	1
Winning Trades	78 (52.70%)
Average Profit %	0.66%
Average Bars Held	1
Maximum Consecutive Winning Trades	8
Losing Trades	70 (47.30%)
Average Loss %	–0.64%
Average Bars Held	0.96
Maximum Consecutive Losing Trades	8

you would be down. Again we see that irrational fear can be exploited with success when people push the market down four days in a row, even in a bear market. Irrational exuberance is not as easy to punish.

However, all hope is not lost, as shown in the next system.

4 UP DAYS AND SHORT FOR 1 PERCENT

- Short when there have been four up days in a row with the last up day being a 2 percent up move. Short on the close.
- Cover either when the position is 1 percent profitable or at the close of the next day.

Example: QQQ, 8/25/99

Square in the middle of the biggest bull run ever, the QQQs made four up days in a row toward the end of the summer of 1999 (see Figure 17.2). The final day of that run was a 2.1 percent up move on August 25. Shorting at the end of that day and waiting for a 1 percent profit would have allowed us to cover at 60.88 the next day.

The results are given in Table 17.4, showing an 86 percent accuracy with an average result of 0.92 percent per trade. Not bad for a one day trade.

TABLE 17.4   4 Up Days and Short for 1%

	All Trades
All Trades	23
Average Profit/Loss %	0.92%
Average Bars Held	1
Winning Trades	20 (86.96%)
Average Profit %	1.21%
Average Bars Held	1
Maximum Consecutive Winning Trades	11
Losing Trades	3 (13.04%)
Average Loss %	−1.01%
Average Bars Held	1
Maximum Consecutive Losing Trades	1

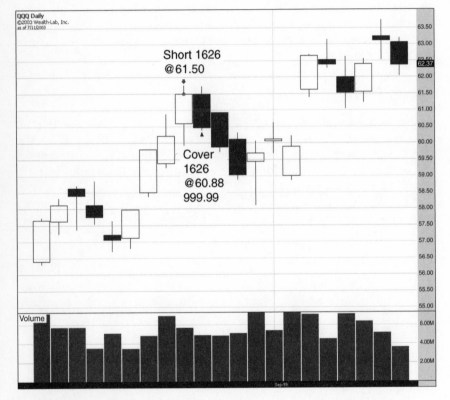

FIGURE 17.2 QQQ on August 25, 1999.

THE 4 PERCENT BREAKOUT MOVE

Day traders and hedge fund managers love to fade sharp moves, particularly sharp up moves. The market moving up ferociously midday is the worst thing for the average hedge fund manager. Why is that? The refrain I constantly hear on those days is, "It's like 1999 again." It is a big party, every stock is going up, the old mutual funds are making a ton of money. It is one of the few days where those funds are probably making more money than the hedge funds. So what does all the smart money try to do then? Well, they try to short and fade the greed. And on a 4 percent up day, this strategy is a big mistake.

The problem is that at the 4 percent point, everyone is looking around and saying, "It can't possibly go any higher." So people jump in on the short side, and when it starts moving higher, a panic results as people try to cover their short positions.

The 4 Percent Breakout System

- Buy QQQ when it hits 4 percent higher than the close the day before.
- Sell at the open the next day.

The results of applying the system to QQQ for March 24, 1999 to June 30, 2003, are listed in Table 17.5, which shows a 63 percent accuracy rate with 0.77 percent profit per trade.

Example: QQQ, 7/5/02

Figure 17.3 is a 30-minute chart of July 5 and July 6, 2002. Before July 4, the markets were in a constant state of panic that there would be a terrorist

TABLE 17.5 4% Breakout

	All Trades
All Trades	124
Average Profit/Loss %	0.77%
Average Bars Held	1
Winning Trades	79 (63.71%)
Average Profit %	2.41%
Average Bars Held	1
Maximum Consecutive Winning Trades	8
Losing Trades	45 (36.29%)
Average Loss %	−2.11%
Average Bars Held	1
Maximum Consecutive Losing Trades	6

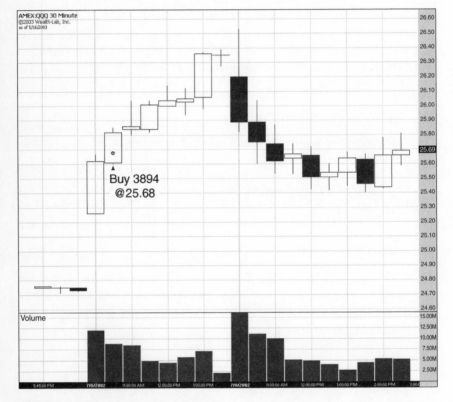

FIGURE 17.3   QQQ on July 5/8, 2002.

attack on the 4th. Everyone was mass dumping their stocks. I called three different brokers to see what their clients were doing, and all said that their clients were convinced that a terrorist attack was going to happen so they were getting the hell out of the stock market. Why they waited until two days before if they were convinced of this I do not understand. Nothing happened, and all the people who had hedged their long portfolios were now stuck with shorts and nowhere to go but cover. So cover they did.

By 10:15 AM on July 5 we were already at the 4 percent point. The market had closed on July 3 at 24.75. At 10:15 AM the system triggered a buy signal 4 percent higher at 25.74 and then sold for a 1.79 percent profit at 26.20 at the open the next day.

A Variation of the 4% Breakout System

A slight improvement is to add the following variation:

- Buy when QQQ is 4 percent higher than the close the day before *and* the day before was down more than 2 percent on the day.
- Sell at the open the next day

See Table 17.6 for the results, which are much better, having a 75 percent accuracy and an average profit of 1.86 percent per trade.

TABLE 17.6 4% Breakout Variation

	All Trades
All Trades	33
Average Profit/Loss %	1.86%
Average Bars Held	1
Winning Trades	25 (75.76%)
Average Profit %	3.31%
Average Bars Held	1
Maximum Consecutive Winning Trades	5
Losing Trades	8 (24.24%)
Average Loss %	−2.68%
Average Bars Held	1
Maximum Consecutive	2

CONCLUSION

The 4 percent breakout system is one of the few times where the principles of mean reversion are basically out the window. Too many people are attempting to fade the move. Consequently, the move proves to be unfadable.

For an example of the 4 percent breakout system applied to South Sea Company stock, see under *Famous First Bubbles* in Technique 20.

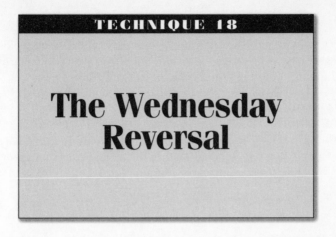

The Wednesday Reversal

There is a saying that the "the dumb money invests in the beginning of the week and the smart money invests at the end." It does turn out that Wednesday is a statistically significant day for reversals to occur.

THE WEDNESDAY WIDE-RANGE MIDWEEK REVERSAL

Price momentum cannot sustain itself for too long in either direction. There are all sorts of reasons for this fact, but the primary one is that people simply get exhausted. Suppose there is nonstop selling for 10 days in a row. At that point it seems like the world is ending. It seems like the only smart thing left to do is sell some more. Well, who is left to sell? The only holders of stocks left are strong holders who have withstood the dips and might even be buying more.

Often the week starts off with some momentum in one direction or other. However, the stronger that momentum is at the beginning of the week, the more likely it is to reverse. Wednesday, dead center in the middle of the week, is the likely candidate day for the reversal.

The System

- Buy QQQ when the low of Tuesday is 5 percent less than the high from Monday (the wide-range condition) and the low of Tuesday is less than the low from Monday. Buy at the open on Wednesday.
- Sell QQQ when two consecutive up closes occur. Sell at the close of the second day.

Note that in the buy conditions we are not requiring that Tuesday actually be a negative day. It could be that the selling has been spent by mid-Tuesday and has already begun to reverse.

Examples

QQQ, 5/24/2001   On Monday, May 22, 2001, the high was 82.25, the low was 75.58. The next day the low was 74.25, over 10 percent less. Buying at the open on Wednesday, May 24 (Figure 18.1), at 75.00 and holding for the close of the second consecutive up day would have allowed you to sell at 93.62 on June 2, 2000 for a 24 percent profit.

Why do we wait for two consecutive up closes? After such a wide range in the early part of the week, the selling has become exhausted. More often than not, with Monday being down a decent range, Tuesday is often worse due to margin calls that must be met. People start to get nervous that the carnage is going to continue all week, so they attempt to bail before it really gets painful. With the range so large, the selling does not usually stop with a whimper, but with a bang. When people realize the worst is not over (with the first up day, usually that Wednesday), they jump back in, causing more than one up day in a row.

QQQ, 10/30/02   Monday October 28, 2002, the high was 25.04 and the low was 24.17. The market had just come off a ferocious rally beginning on October 9 and people were still skeptical. So, after a weekend to think about it, they took a break from the buying. The market continued to sell off on Tuesday with a low at 23.37. Although Tuesday was a down day with a close at 23.92, it is interesting to note that we were almost 3 percent off of the lows. Buying the gap up on Wednesday morning, October 30 (Figure 18.2), at 24.06 would have caused you some initial worry when it dipped back down to 23.85 before closing 2 percent higher at 24.56. Finally, the second consecutive up close occurred a week later on November 4 and you would have sold at 25.90 for a 7.64 percent profit.

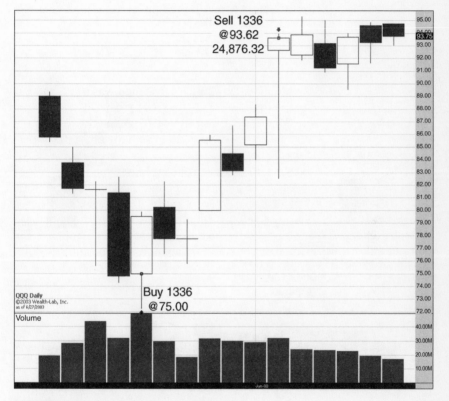

FIGURE 18.1 QQQ on May 24, 2001.

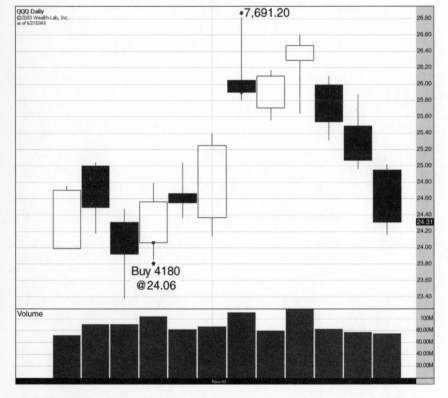

FIGURE 18.2   QQQ on October 30, 2002.

Results

Table 18.1 shows the results of applying this system to QQQ trading March 24, 1999 to June 30, 2003. You can see an average profit of 3.20 percent per trade with 70 percent accuracy.

TABLE 18.1 Wednesday Reversal	
	All Trades
All Trades	52
Average Profit/Loss %	3.20%
Average Bars Held	3.77
Winning Trades	36 (69.23%)
Average Profit %	6.05%
Average Bars Held	2.5
Maximum Consecutive Winning Trades	6
Losing Trades	16 (30.77%)
Average Loss %	−3.21%
Average Bars Held	6.63
Maximum Consecutive Losing Trades	2

Wide-Range System (non-Wednesday)

Is the Wednesday condition critical? If we apply the same system but only when the wide range occurs on any two days other than Monday–Tuesday, we get the results shown in Table 18.2.

TABLE 18.2 Wide-Range (Not Wednesday)	
	All Trades
All Trades	80
Average Profit/Loss %	0.90%
Average Bars Held	5.09
Winning Trades	48 (60.00%)
Average Profit %	4.49%
Average Bars Held	3.6
Maximum Consecutive Winning Trades	9
Losing Trades	32 (40.00%)
Average Loss %	−4.50%
Average Bars Held	7.31
Maximum Consecutive Losing Trades	5

We can see this is definitely a playable system, with a 60 percent accuracy rate and an average profit of 0.90 percent per trade. However, note that the average bars held, 5.09, is greater than the average bars held for the Wednesday version, which is 3.77. The profit per bar is significantly less in the non-Wednesday system: 0.17 percent per bar versus 0.84 percent per bar in the Wednesday version. Typically, I like to have an expected value of at least 0.40 percent per day before I consider a system playable given that the reality is usually much less when taking into account commissions and slippage.

If we add the condition (in the Wednesday version) that Tuesday be a down day, the results get better but not better enough that I'd be willing to *only* play this system when Tuesday down. With Tuesday down the results are 33 out of 44, with an average profit per trade of 3.40 percent. An improvement, but not good enough to become a mandatory condition.

THE WIDE-RANGE MIDWEEK REVERSAL SYSTEM APPLIED TO STOCKS

The wide-range system can also be applied to stocks. First, though, rather than use a static interpretation of what is defined as a wide range, let us borrow the concept of the average true range of the stock. The average true range is defined by Welles Wilder in his 1978 book, *New Concepts in Technical Trading Systems* (Trend Research, 1978), as:

- The current high less the current low.
- The absolute value of: current high less the previous close.
- The absolute value of: current low less the previous close.

On large range days, the first condition usually applies. On days that gap up, the second condition will usually apply. And on days that gap down, the third condition will usually apply. The average true range (ATR) is then the average over some specified period of the true ranges. We will use an ATR over a 10-day period.

The System

- Buy a stock when the Tuesday low is ($1.5 \times$ ATR of the past 10 days) less than the Monday high (the range is 50 percent higher than its average range) and the Tuesday low is less than the Monday low. Buy the open on Wednesday.
- Sell when there have been two consecutive up closes.

Examples

PIXR, 7/24/02   PIXR (and the market in general) was going through a horrendous July in 2002. After three down days from Wednesday to Friday the week before, Monday July 22, reached a high of 41.92 before closing at 40.00, and the low on Tuesday reached 39.17, staking out a range of 7 percent between those two days. A buy signal was triggered for Wednesday, July 24 (Figure 18.3), at 39.11. Wednesday was an up day, as was Thursday. So the system exited the trade at the close on Thursday at 41.88 for a profit of 9.47 percent.

USAI, 2/5/03   Monday, February 3, 2003, USAI went from a high of 22.58 to close near its low at 21.88. The next day the stock gapped down and continued to fall further, hitting a low of 20.73 before closing at 20.99. The next day, Wednesday, February 5 (Figure 18.4, page 197), the system buys at the open of 21.68. Note that although Wednesday closed down from the open, it was still an up day, closing at 21.34. So it was the first up day, with Thursday then being the second consecutive up day, closing at 23.21 where the system sells for a 7 percent profit.

Results

For the results of applying this system to all Nasdaq 100 stocks for June 30, 1998, to June 30, 2003, including deletions from the Index during that period, see Table 18.3.

TABLE 18.3   Wednesday Reversal Applied to NAS 100 Stocks

	All Trades
All Trades	5,802
Average Profit/Loss %	2.59%
Average Bars Held	5.04
Winning Trades	3886 (66.98%)
Average Profit %	7.87%
Average Bars Held	3.28
Maximum Consecutive Winning Trades	42
Losing Trades	1916 (33.02%)
Average Loss %	−8.31%
Average Bars Held	8.51
Maximum Consecutive Losing Trades	16

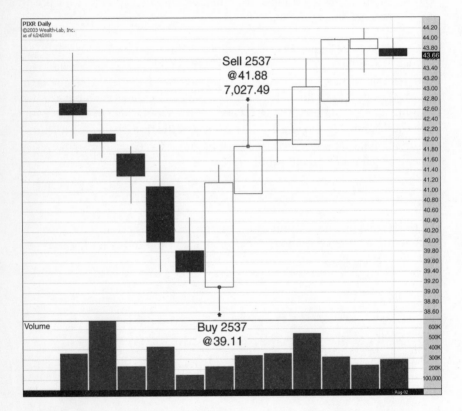

FIGURE 18.3   PIXR on July 24, 2002.

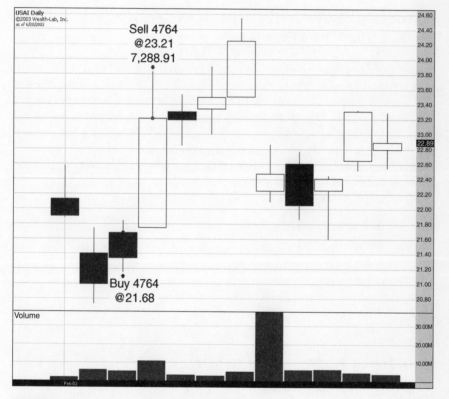

FIGURE 18.4 USAI on February 5, 2003.

Simulation

Figure 18.5 shows a simulation using 2 percent of equity per trade. I wanted to see how many of the weeks were profitable. The top bars represent profitable weeks; the bottom bars represent unprofitable weeks. Out of 260 weeks, 175 were profitable, with the average return per week at 0.76 percent and a standard deviation of 3.07.

SHORTING WITH THE WIDE-RANGE WEDNESDAY REVERSAL

As has been demonstrated throughout this book, shorting is just not a winning strategy in either bull or bear markets. Many short-selling funds even produced negative results in 2001 because of the huge spike that occurred on January 3, 2001, due to the first interest-rate cut. A 5 percent move in the markets is enough to cause serious damage to a short-selling fund where the risk of loss is unlimited. However, when people are extra giddy in the early part of the week, the market likes to take a little back, and the potential for reversal is highest on a Wednesday.

The Wednesday Short System

- Short when Tuesday's close is 1 percent higher than Friday's close and Wednesday's open is higher than Tuesday's close. Short the open on Wednesday.
- Cover on the second close of two consecutive down closes.

Examples

QQQ, March 7, 2001   Friday, March 2, 2001, the QQQs closed at 46.70, followed by two days that both gapped up but closed somewhat flattish with their opens. Tuesday closed at 49.40, 5.7 percent higher than the Friday close and then proceeded to gap up another several percent. Wednesday morning, March 7 (Figure 18.6, page 200), when QQQ opened at 50.40, 50.40 turned out to be the high of the day. Shorting then and covering after two consecutive down closes resulted in a cover on Friday at the close at 45.10 for a profit of 10.52 percent. Note that although Wednesday was down from open to close, it actually was a positive day for QQQ over the Tuesday close since it closed on that Wednesday at 49.42, 2 cents higher than the Tuesday close but already a nice profit for the system.

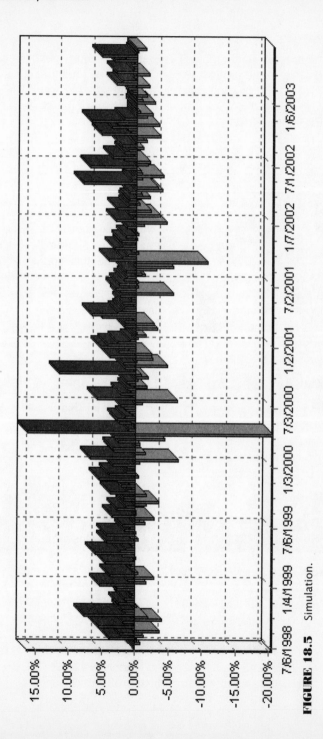

FIGURE 18.5 Simulation.

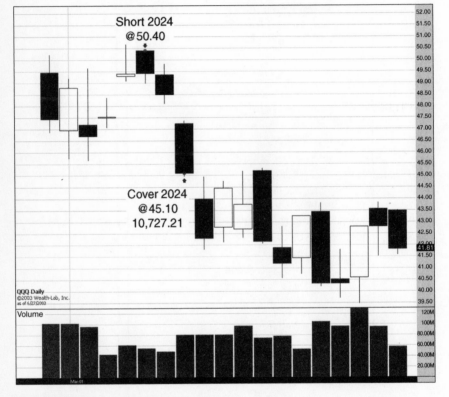

FIGURE 18.6 QQQ on March 7, 2001.

QQQ, November 6, 2002   As seen in a previous example, Wednesday, October 30, 2002, had triggered the wide-range Wednesday reversal system. Although that system sold QQQ for a nice profit on the Thursday close, the market continued to rally with three more consecutive up closes. The QQQs closed on Friday, November 1, at 25.25 and then had two more up closes before closing on Tuesday, November, 5 at 26.10, several percent higher.

Wednesday, the 5th (Figure 18.7), the QQQs gapped higher, opening at 26.29 and continuing higher, closing at 26.47 despite dipping as low as 25.64 during the day. The dip was a foreshadowing of things to come as the next two days the market gapped lower before the trade was closed out at the close on Friday at 25.07 for a 4.64 percent profit.

Results

See Table 18.4 for results of the Wednesday QQQ short system, March 24, 1999 to June 30, 2003. The table shows a 1.87 percent average profit per trade with an accuracy of 2/3.

The greater Tuesday is higher than Friday's close, the better the system works. For instance, instead of looking for Tuesdays that are 1 percent higher than Friday's close, if we look for Tuesdays that are 2 percent higher, we get the results shown in Table 18.5 (see page 203). The accuracy improves to 72 percent and the average profit per trade goes to 2.04 percent.

The system also works fine if you change the Wednesday condition to any day but Wednesday. See Table 18.6 (see page 203). The accuracy stays largely the same, but profit per trade goes down significantly.

TABLE 18.4   Wednesday QQQ Short

	All Trades
All Trades	33
Average Profit/Loss %	1.87%
Average Bars Held	5.21
Winning Trades	22 (66.67%)
Average Profit %	4.66%
Average Bars Held	2.64
Maximum Consecutive Winning Trades	6
Losing Trades	11 (33.33%)
Average Loss %	−3.72%
Average Bars Held	10.36
Maximum Consecutive Losing Trades	3

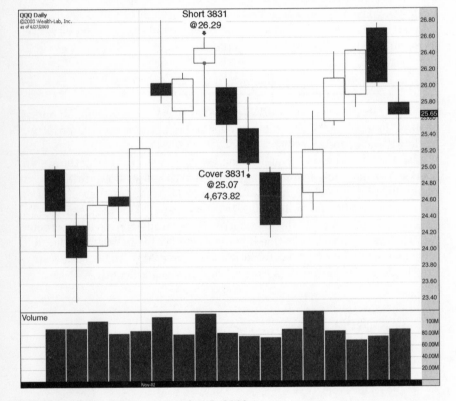

FIGURE 18.7   QQQ on November 6, 2002.

TABLE 18.5 Wednesday QQQ Short—Variation

	All Trades
All Trades	25
Average Profit/Loss %	2.04%
Average Bars Held	4.12
Winning Trades	18 (72.00%)
Average Profit %	4.35%
Average Bars Held	2.39
Maximum Consecutive Winning Trades	9
Losing Trades	7 (28.00%)
Average Loss %	−3.90%
Average Bars Held	8.57
Maximum Consecutive Losing Trades	2

TABLE 18.6 Wednesday QQQ Short—Variation

	All Trades
All Trades	80
Average Profit/Loss %	0.89%
Average Bars Held	5.22
Winning Trades	53 (66.25%)
Average Profit %	3.53%
Average Bars Held	3.74
Maximum Consecutive Winning Trades	10
Losing Trades	27 (33.75%)
Average Loss %	−4.28%
Average Bars Held	8.15
Maximum Consecutive Losing Trades	3

CONCLUSION

Basically, it is not the case that Wednesday is the only day one can do a reversal trade. But it is certainly the best day by a long shot and makes the most intuitive sense. Momentum is hard to sustain for a straight week, so it makes sense that the middle of the week is the time when momentum breaks down.

It is worth spending time testing variations of the Wednesday system. As an example of the type of exhaustion that tends to occur on Wednesday, consider the following pattern:

- Short when QQQ is gapping up between 0.5 percent and 1.5 percent, the open today is less than the open yesterday, and it is Wednesday.
- Cover on 0.5 percent profit, or at the close if not profitable.

So, in other words, we are getting a big gap up, the market is excited, but despite the size of the gap, the market is still not going to open higher than the open was yesterday. The result is 17 of 17 successful trades with an average profit of 0.5 percent per trade.

While it might often seem like the end of the world on a Tuesday evening, or the beginning of the next humongous bull market, you can be safely assured that Wednesdays often play the role of the Great Humiliator and set these thoughts to rest. By patiently waiting for these moments and fading whatever trend started in the beginning of the week, one can have a high probability of a profitable second half of the week.

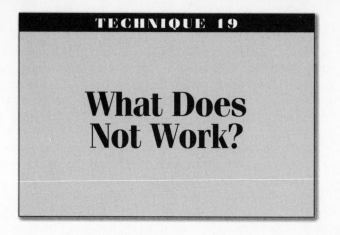

TECHNIQUE 19

What Does Not Work?

I would assume that most people reading this book have also read many other investment books recommending various systems and techniques for "beating the market." In Technique 20 I recommend my favorite books and you can take or leave that list with a grain of salt. Each person has his or her own style and approach and should find the support to suit that approach. My own personal opinion is that knowing the history, science, and art of any field in which you seek to become one of the top 1 percent of players is critical for success.

When Bobby Fischer was 13 years old, he was an above-average chess player but certainly not someone who seemed destined to become the world champion and, perhaps, the greatest player ever. At that time he basically disappeared for about a year or so and did an intensive study of the games of Wilhelm Steinitz, the world chess champion of the last twenty years of the 1800s. Why did Fischer do this? In terms of technique the games were outdated. The openings Steinitz played were rarely used in modern tournament play, even in the 1950s when Fischer was a teenager. And yet, by studying those games, finding flaws where prior annotators had not, and doing a detailed analysis of the techniques, Fischer was able to improve his play to an extent that at the age of 15 he was suddenly the youngest U.S. champion ever, as well as the youngest grandmaster ever. In addition, he taught himself enough Russian so he could read the Soviet magazine, *64*, which contained analyses from Russian grandmasters over the latest opening theory. By combining a scientific study of the history of chess with intense research into the modern techniques of the day, he was able to so clearly surpass his colleagues that from the age of 15, until perhaps even now, they have never been able to touch him. That is the story of mastery in a nutshell.

Chess is a game, and there is very little money attached to being good at that particular game. Often, when a child becomes an adult, the pleasures of games move to the background and other endeavors take over. When it comes to making money for yourself, for your family, or for your clients, the competition is unbounded. There are hundreds of thousands of investors from all over the world every day trying to take money from you. Disregarding the argument of whether it is a zero-sum game, clearly it is better for your competitors if you lose money and they make money. Nobody will feel bad if you get wiped out. Others will move up to take your place. And every day investors get wiped out. The Yahoo! message boards are littered with these people. As well as the halls of Nobel Prize winners and people who are successful in other fields that now turn their attention toward investing and find that success now eludes them.

In this book I mention a few of the techniques that I have used and will continue to use to make money for myself and my clients. I highly recommend that people test for themselves these techniques both through research and through active trading. I am confident that they will stand up to the test. That said, I also think it is important for people to research their own ideas and also to learn what does not work. Along with keeping a detailed and catalogued database of the techniques and patterns that I have tested that work, I also keep track of patterns and ideas that do not work. Following are a few of those ideas

GUT

"The market feels like it's going down from here." Perhaps the best feeling a beginning trader can have is that feeling she gets when she senses the market is going to go up, she buys, and, like magic, it goes up. Note that I said "beginning trader." This technique of relying on feeling does not work. It has never worked for anybody. Perhaps the best tape reader ever, Jesse Livermore, died bankrupt at the receiving end of his own gun. Yes, it can work 9 times out of 10. Amazing streaks can happen. But the 10th time you will lose everything. You. Will. Lose. Everything. If you are not a serious investor but spend much time talking to your broker, ask yourself if he is trading based on his gut. I have nothing against brokers, but *The Making of a Stock Broker* by Edwin Lefevre (Fraser, reprinted in 1999), written in the early 1900s, sums it all up. Do not trade on gut or listen to anybody who does.

CONFIRMATION

In many of the techniques described in this book you will be buying stocks or the market as they are going down, or shorting/selling them as they are going up. In other words, buying low and selling high. Can they get lower? Sure. In fact, most of the time they will. Many books out there suggest an alternative to this approach: why not buy stocks *after* they hit bottom and already start to move up? I can smack myself in the head! Why didn't I think of that?!

For instance, suppose a stock gaps down below the prior day's low. Why not just buy the stock after it hits bottom and goes back over the prior day's low? Not only that, you can even buy it higher like when it goes back through the prior day's low and passes it by one or two ticks. This is real confirmation that it is going to move up, according to many of the authors out there. In my own tests on this particular idea and other similar ones, I have not found this so-called confirmation to be the case. The higher up you buy in many situations, the more money you have left on the table (or the more money you have lost).

I do not mean to make light of the technique of waiting for confirmation. It does have the appearance of being cautious compared with "catching a falling knife." However, with proper testing and research you can time your purchases to have much better results than if the market or a stock has already bounced several percent back up. I do believe the techniques recommended in many great investing books have perhaps been successful in the past. But since the late 1990s there are many more players in the game. The hedge fund world has gone from 100 hedge funds averaging $5M each to 5000 hedge funds averaging $100M each. Prop trading shops with hundreds of day traders in each one have popped up all over the country. Many more people day trade from their homes. These people are not letting you wait for confirmation.

On the Web site RealMoney.com, the excellent columnist "Rev Shark" has brought up a very good point, however. It could be the case that excellent money management lessens the pain in many systems that cannot be as thoroughly researched as others. For instance, many technical analysis techniques require some degree of subjectivity to identify the patterns that are appearing in the market. Using a method to limit losses is critical, particularly if part of one's plan is to use trading techniques that are not backed up by rigorous research.

CANDLESTICK PATTERNS

I have really enjoyed Steve Nison's books on Japanese candlesticks and highly recommend them to anyone interested in learning more about these basic market patterns. I also think that for many years these techniques worked in the markets, but they simply do not work anymore. If anything, so many people anticipate the effects of the candlestick patterns and attempt to game them that often the reverse of what is predicted by the particular pattern ends up happening. That said, an invaluable way to gain a deeper understanding of the markets is to test every candlestick pattern out there and see for yourself.

SEASONALITY

The Stock Trader's Almanac by Yale and Jeffrey Hirsch (Wiley, 2003), is one of my favorite books. Each year it comes out with new information, new quotes, new ideas for how the market responds throughout the year to different events. Seasonality does work if you can identify a seasonal pattern before anyone else does. However, I think this is largely impossible. What ends up happening is that as soon as someone realizes that every year the day before Memorial Day is up, then everyone realizes it. Then using seasonality as a system no longer works—too many people anticipating it. A great example is the January effect. Once people realized the January effect (the tendency over the past 80 years for the markets to go up in January) was real, they started buying in December. It became the December effect. Now it has become more like the October effect with huge up moves in recent Octobers. By the time this book is out, it might be the September effect. Who knows? Another seasonal-based idea is "Sell in May and Go Away." Well, as of this writing anybody who followed the strategy would have missed out on 100 percent moves in many stocks this year.

LOW P/E, HIGH P/E

Believe me when I say I am not trashing fundamentals. If one is a buy and hold investor, then the best strategy you can use is to find undervalued companies that are growing (this part is key), buy them, and look at them every two or three years. Truly the way to riches is to somehow identify the next Microsoft or Berkshire Hathaway and ride it all the way to the top. As ludicrous as this sounds (and I cannot claim to know how to do this), some people did do it and made themselves millionaires many times over.

At the 2003 Berkshire Hathaway annual meeting, I met a guy who bought 200 shares of Berkshire in 1976 for around $70 a share. He told me that a year later, when the stock had doubled, he sold half his position. Great trade—100 percent in a year. Now his remaining 100 shares are worth $7.5M. I asked him why he bought the shares in the first place. He had heard about Warren Buffett's successes in Buffett's hedge fund. He liked the insurance business and trends in the insurance business, and he just decided to make a bet. That's it. Nothing fancy. Did he get lucky? Sure he did. But his story is a great example of how buy and hold can work.

So what does this story have to do with P/E? Answer: nothing. P/E really has no use when it comes to valuing a company. I highly recommend that people check out the Forbes article written by Ken Fisher titled, "The P/E myth" for more on this topic. The article can be found on the Web at http://www.forbes.com/global/2002/1111/074asia.html.

WCOM had a P/E in the low single digits when it was revealed that it was corrupt to the tune of several billion dollars and ended up filing bankruptcy. Many deep-value investors were writing articles at the time about what a great buy WCOM was because of its low P/E. And many high P/E stocks continued to flourish in both earnings and stock price throughout the recent bear market, eBay being the best example. Building a market-neutral portfolio of long low P/E stocks and short high P/E stocks is probably the quickest way to personal bankruptcy, and I do not recommend it as an investing technique. If it were that easy to invest then everyone would be rich.

But shouldn't a company be valued based on its future cash flows? Yes, I certainly believe this. But don't look at lagging P/Es to determine those future cash flows. Instead, analyze demographic trends about where the customers are coming from for different industries. Warren Buffett is not buying Dairy Queen, manufactured housing companies, convenience store distribution companies, and such because of their price over cash flows, but because we have an ever-increasing lower middle class in the United States so that regardless of the economy, his customer base for these companies is going to increase. Companies like Allergan, the maker of Botox, have not gone up this year because of their current cash flows (although they hope that those cash flows are growing), but because the number of new customers in their target demographic (women age 45–55) is increasing by one million every year regardless of the economy.

Was the Internet a bubble? There certainly was an IPO bubble as investment banks continued to pump out supplies of shares even after demand for those shares had topped out. But the reality is that the demographic of Internet users went from 0 commercial users to 300M around the world in fewer than five years, and some companies (eBay, Yahoo!, etc.) stood to benefit and will continue to benefit.

In addition to the trends mentioned above which I still feel are only in their beginning stages there is also the trend of technology now being outsourced to India, Malaysia, Singapore, and, eventually, China. As opposed to the United States, these countries also have large birthrates that guarantee that the number of people from the ages of 20 to 40 supporting the number of people hitting the age of 70+ will stay at a healthy ratio. Who will benefit? Who will lose? Focus on solving this puzzle, not doing a Yahoo! finance search on companies with low P/E. That approach will not make you money.

BUYING AND SELLING OPTIONS

People buy options because they want leverage on their purchases. People sell options because they want income. You should not do either. If you can consistently pick successful stocks, then you do not need leverage thanks to the miraculous power of compounding. And the idea of making income by selling naked calls or covered calls is a lot more complicated than popular authors would lead you to believe. The commonly told lie is that 90 percent of options expire worthless, so you might as well sell them all day long and pocket the money from selling them before they go to zero. For the sake of your own personal sanity, stop these efforts, particularly without testing and research. Sophisticated arbitrage strategies using options do work, but they do not work for dilettantes.

CONCLUSION

OK, enough negativity from me. I do think that the investing world is very big and that many, many techniques can work if followed with the appropriate discipline and money management. There is no shortage of players out there, each playing his or her particular strategies: mutual funds that buy and hold, hedge funds that trend follow, short sellers that provide liquidity, and so on. If you have a technique that, through testing, you feel will work, there will be no shortage of players who will take the opposite side of your trade.

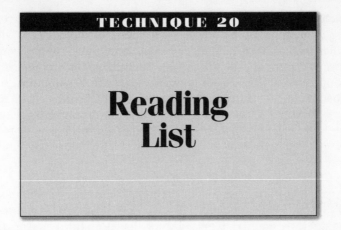

TECHNIQUE 20

Reading
List

In every sport, science, art, or game (and arguably trading and investing have elements of all four) it takes years of sacrifice and endeavor to achieve the highest levels of proficiency and success. In investing, the rewards are so great and the competition so fierce that you have to be aware that anything less than 12 hours a day for years and years will guarantee that you will never achieve those rewards.

Much has been written about achieving mastery in a topic. Clearly, talent is an important factor, but it is, perhaps, the least important. Usually people who achieve mastery in a topic cite several different reasons for their success:

- Incessant practice. When Michael Jordan failed to make his high school basketball team, he practiced shooting every day until he knew that he would not experience that failure again. Anatoly Karpov, former world champion in chess, spent eight hours a day studying the game for eight solid years before achieving grandmaster strength.
- Thorough knowledge of the history of your field. Every great artist has studied the works of the masters from the past 10 centuries. Every great chess player can recite the games of Paul Morphy, the world champion from the mid-1800s, by heart. In investing, knowing the history of ideas, studying the rises and falls of the market since its inception, and reading the biographies of the great investors over the past decade cannot help but improve your ability to survive the current markets. Studying in detail the masters who have come before you is critical in any venture at all. I really believe the only way you can end up

developing, testing, and cultivating your own opinions and ideas is on top of the foundations built by the others before you.

- Ability to deal with failure. The only people who do not win in this game are the ones who quit. IASG, the Institutional Advisory Services Group, maintains a Web site tracking all of the top commodity trading advisors (CTAs): http://iasg.pertrac2000.com. I like to check this Web site occasionally to see how all the competition is doing. One time I came across a fund that was down 22 percent its first year of business and only up 3 percent in its second year. I cannot imagine the pain those guys must have gone through. But 18 years later Dunn Capital is one of the biggest CTAs in the database with over $1B in assets and an annualized return of almost 20 percent. There are countless examples out there of hedge fund managers who sat through painful drawdowns but stuck to their systems, did not deviate, and managed to come through the other side with amazing success both for themselves and their clients.

That being said, I am providing the following reading list made up of books I have enjoyed and that I feel have helped me to help you on your path to mastery as well. Some of them are about investing; others are only peripherally related and may not suit your tastes or interests. But I have included the reasons why each one helped me in investing so you can decide how each might be useful to you.

Practical Speculation (Wiley, 2003) and *Education of a Speculator* (Wiley, 1998) by Victor Niederhoffer

I really cannot say enough about these two books. How often can you get advice about investing from a guy who has been involved in every aspect of investing over the past 40 years? Not to mention that he was world squash champ for 10 of those years, achieving a level of success in two fields when I would be happy to achieve it in just one. In addition to being a researcher, a pit trader, a trader for Soros, a hedge fund manager, and an owner of an M&A business for 20 years, he has also been an excellent writer in the markets, writing each week for MSN, still testing new ideas and asking new questions about the markets whenever he can.

The most important idea in these books is the notion that one needs to test everything. This is no small matter. Often the media makes gross claims like:

- "When P/Es are high, the markets go down"
- "Stock XYZ just crossed above its 200-day moving average, which is very bullish."

- "The market is forming a head and shoulders pattern, which is very bearish."

And the list goes on. Regardless of whether any of these statements are true (none of them are), they are all testable. Many of the investment books I have read since the early 1990s have recommended systems that did not stand up under basic testing. Why is this? I honestly cannot tell you. Even if one wants to trade on gut and not using a systematic method, basic testing will help build intuition by simply showing you the facts about what has worked in the past and what has not.

Practical Speculation contains chapters on how to identify spurious correlations to more "fun" topics such as: Has Alan Abelson *ever* been bullish on the markets?

Confessions of a Street Addict (Simon & Schuster, 2002) by Jim Cramer

Jim Cramer often gets a bum rap. He is high energy and it shows when he is on CNBC on Kudlow & Cramer. He has single-handedly popularized the concept that individual investors can invest for themselves and not hand all their money to the often incompetent people at brokerage houses or mutual funds. The Web sites he has started through thestreet.com umbrella have become the best brands in online financial journalism. (I am biased, of course, since I write for them.)

At the end of the day, it is hard to beat Cramer's track record. For the years he was in business, he returned a solid 30 percent a year—very legit and hard for anyone to beat. And yet what stands out in his book are not his successes, but his brushes with failure. His first week in business he was down nearly 10 percent and almost had to shut down. And then again in mid-1998 he was down 20 percent year to date. Being a hedge fund manager and learning to survive those periods are critical to success. The 1998 chapter is a classic.

One thing that stands out to me about both Jim Cramer and Victor Niederhoffer is that both responded to my initial e-mails despite having no idea who I was or any reason to write back to me. For those gestures I am grateful and hope to be able to emulate at least some of their successes.

Market Wizards (Harper Business, 1994), *The New Market Wizards* (Harper Business, 1994), *Stock Market Wizards* (Harper Business, 2003) by Jack Schwager

I am a sucker for biographies and interviews with people in whatever field I am interested in. All three of Schwager's books have some excellent interviews, and almost every interview has some takeaway that can help an investor. My favorite interviews in the books were:

- Monroe Trout. His technique is all about testing patterns in the market for statistical significance. I strongly believe in this approach and have probably reread this interview no fewer than 20 times. I also like his approach to money management and capping his losses per trade and month at fixed amounts.
- Gil Blake. I am not a big fan of mutual fund timing, but in his interview Blake mentions the idea that he just needs to create systems with positive expected value and then make as many trades as possible in those systems. His quote on diversification: "If the odds are 70 percent in your favor and you make 50 trades, it's very difficult to have a down year." The key, I guess, is getting the odds 70 percent in your favor.
- Mark Cook. Some of Cook's ideas on the tick inspired me to start looking at it for my own trading, some of the results of which appear in this book.

These are just a few of the interviews but, again, all of them had some takeaway that I found useful.

SuperMoney (Warner Books, 1973) and *The Money Game* (Random House, 1976) by Adam Smith

I love pop finance books from the 1970s. In particular, these investment books by Adam Smith have never gone out of date. For instance, in one of the books, I forget which, he mentions a friend calling him and saying a major bank is about to collapse due to some problem with derivatives. This was written thirty years ago and on a daily basis I still hear this rumor.

In *SuperMoney* he also pals around Omaha with then-unknown investor Warren Buffett. Buffett at the time had about $40M and was trying to figure out what to do with his life. While they were driving around, Buffett pointed at the Nebraska Furniture Mart and said, "Someday I'm going to own that." The rest is history.

In the very next chapter, Smith provides the details of a Swiss bank he invested in that went bankrupt, and the founder ended up spending time in jail. The founder, Paul Erdmann, went on to become one of the most successful financial thriller writers ever. I highly recommend his first book, *The Billion Dollar Sure Thing* (Berkeley Publishing, reprint, 1988).

Along these lines of 1970s pop finance books is Andrew Tobias's book, *The Funny Money Game* (Playboy, 1972), detailing the rise and fall of National Student Marketing, the high P/E growth stock that he was in the management of. If ever there was a dot-com before the late 1990s, this was it. And it also shows that the Internet bubble was not the first of its kind, nor will it be the last. Again, these books from the 1970s are great examples of how things never change.

Tomorrow's Gold (LSA, 2002) by Marc Faber

Just reading this book by Faber is going to raise your IQ. This guy knows his history, in every market in every country that's ever existed. The book is basically about emerging markets and the cycles that make up an emerging market. He details how events such as the Internet boom and even the railroad boom of the 1800s and other periods of technological innovation had many of the characteristics of an emerging market. The book weaves together demographics, history, and a global macro understanding of today's markets to put together a consistent investment thesis. At the very least, after reading this book you will be able to talk intelligently at cocktail parties about the Asian markets.

Famous First Bubbles (MIT, 2000) by Peter Garber

This is a small book that describes in detail the Tulipmania bubble and the Mississippi and South Sea bubbles. Like a similar book, *Devil Take the Hindmost* (Plume, reprint, 2000) by [Peter Gruber], *Famous First Bubbles* describes the history but also provides a breakdown of the fundamentals of each bubble, which demonstrates that these bubbles were perhaps not bubbles. For instance, in the case of the South Sea Company, as crooked as the company was, the fundamentals might have justified higher prices. However, encouraged by the success of South Sea, many other fly-by-night operations were going public and encouraging massive overspeculation until finally the whole thing collapsed. Sounds like another recent bubble. (Or was it a bubble?)

I tried two different systems described in this book to see what would happen if you applied the techniques here to the stock of the South Sea Company in 1721: the 4 percent system and the Turtle system.

Recall that the 4 percent system buys a stock intraday when it is 4 percent higher than the close the day before. It closes out the position at the end of the day. The idea is that short sellers who are trying to speculate midday are going to get squeezed by the end of the day, causing a run into the close. See Figure A.1, which shows the 4% up system applied to South Sea Company. The results would have been 35 trades, of which 20 would have been successful and had an average profit per trade of 4.71 percent.

Applying the Turtle system described in Technique 7 would also have worked quite well (Figure A.2, page 217), resulting in one trade with a profit of 443 percent within one year. Not bad.

When Genius Failed (Random House, 2000) by Roger Lowenstein

When Genius Failed is like a horror novel. Everyone gets rich, billions of dollars rich, and then it all comes tumbling down while at the same time putting the entire world on the brink of financial collapse. As with

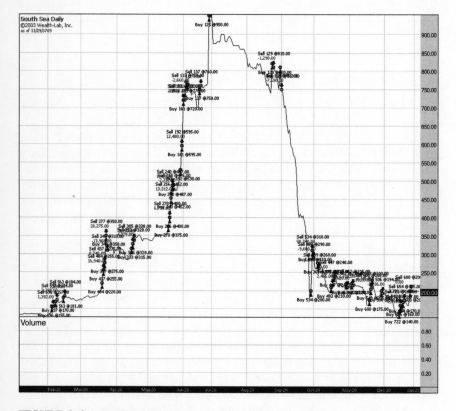

FIGURE A.1   South Sea Company, 1720, 4 percent system.

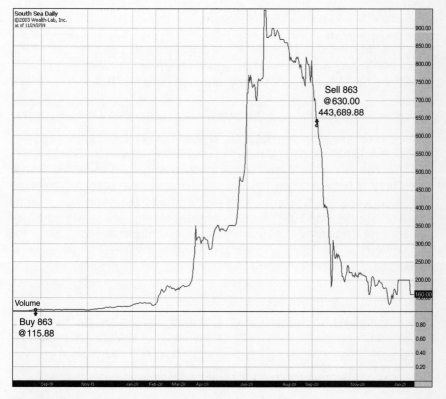

FIGURE A.2 South Sea Company, 1720, slow Turtle system.

anything, it is important to be a skeptic. Keep in mind that the portfolio of LTCM, if left alone, would have had a profitable year. Which is why guys like Warren Buffett were trying to bid for it. The banks had a panic attack that the fund was going to fail and trillions of dollars would be lost and shut everything down. Note that Merriwether's new fund now is supposedly doing very well.

The book and topic has an interesting psychology to it. Most people I have spoken to about LTCM who have read the book seem happy to recount the stories of Nobel Prize winners *failing* and guys losing billions. Failure and loss is not the point of the book or that story at all. The point is, what happened to LTCM can easily happen to you, me, anyone who engages in this field. Constant self-management and being aware of the lessons of history through backtesting and reading books like *When Genius Failed* are the only methods I know of for avoiding this fate.

Triumph of the Optimists (Princeton, 2002) by Dimson, Marsh, Staunton

What was the triumph? The fact that anyone who invested in U.S. equities in 1950 would have had a real return of over 9 percent a year. Unbelievable, particularly since at 1950 many members of the Graham and Dodd school were already believing that U.S. stocks were too expensive. In *Triumph*, the authors analyze the stock, bond, and currency returns of every major country over the past 100 years. To say this is the most important history book for global market investing would be an understatement. Take from this book what you will; my conclusion from the book is to never underestimate the U.S. market.

Reminiscences of a Stock Operator (Wiley, 1994) by Edwin Lefevre

This fictionalized biography of Jesse Livermore is a classic and the one by Lefevre that is commonly quoted, but any book by Lefevre is a must, particularly *Wall Street Stories* (Greenwood, 1901) and *The Making of a Stockbroker* (Fraser, 1999). Like the previously mentioned pop finance books from the 1970s, Lefevre's books underline the fact that even since 100 years ago, nothing has really changed.

The Stock Trader's Almanac (Wiley, 2003) by Yale Hirsch and Jeffrey Hirsch

The *Almanac* is the bible for seasonal investing. It is filled with stats and curiosities about what happens on almost any day, week, month of the year in the markets. There are lots of fun facts that provide insights into the secrets of the market. Personally, I think the Hirsch family has carved out for themselves the funnest job on the planet—data mining the market day and night to find the latest info for the next edition. That said, it is somewhat difficult to trade on seasonal factors. For instance, once everyone knows that Januarys tend to go up, they start buying in December, and so on. The key to taking advantage of any repeating seasonal factor is to recognize that factor before anyone else does—easier said than done.

Moneyball (WW Norton, 2003) by Michael Lewis

Moneyball is the story of Billy Beane and the Oakland As in 2002 when, despite having one of the lowest payrolls in the league, they end up winning more games than any other team in the American League. How did they do it? By using the same techniques described in this book: uncovering statistical anomalies in their market (the market for good baseball players) and using those anomalies to reap profits (win more games). A baseball term such as the "expected run value" that describes how many runs can be expected from a particular diamond situation is strikingly like the "expected value" term used to describe the average profit per trade in a particular system.

Gary Kasparov on My Great Predecessors, Part 1 (Everyman, 2003) by Gary Kasparov

Kasparov is probably the best world champion ever. Of course, we can argue this and say maybe he never surpassed Bobby Fischer at his peak. Or maybe the new blood, Vladmir Kramnik might be better. Who knows? In my opinion, Kasparov is the best. And that he does a detailed study of every world champion preceding him makes the book worth looking at. As I have said before, knowing the history of any field you attempt to master is a critical must.

Index